AGEE.

by

Peter H. Ohlin

IVAN OBOLENSKY, INC. · *New York*

In Memoriam
Per Holger Ohlin
1896–1962

CONTENTS

PREFACE

This book was originally written as a doctoral dissertation at the University of New Mexico. In revising it for publication I have made a number of minor changes. The limited extent of these revisions does not mean that I am satisfied with the book; on the contrary, I find it in many ways painfully inadequate. On the other hand, I do not know how it could possibly be improved without losing what I conceived of as its purpose: as this book will try to show, the works of James Agee demand, above all, a human cooperation, a willingness to respond in terms as broadly and inclusively human as possible, and any effort to present a "definitive" analytical reading of those works is surely just another sign of the kind of official acceptance which Agee himself called "the one unmistakable symptom that salvation is beaten again." Thus, a more academic book would surely be untrue to its subject, and a less academic one might lose all relevance. Finally, of course, the compromise I have attempted is foredoomed, and no minor or major changes could possibly alter this fact. If the present book leads some readers to rediscover Agee, it has served its purpose.

Perhaps the one true alternative to this book that I

could imagine would be the publication *in toto* of a journal of my total experience during the years I dealt intensively with Agee; that is the *kind* of response that would seem most appropriate. But as I did not keep such a journal, that book has been lost. The inadequate compromise I present is the closest I can come to recognizing my own experience; as part of the peculiar world of academic enterprises, my immediate response to Agee and his works was necessarily colored by my awareness of scholarly methods and my acceptance of such academic conventions as footnotes and bibliographies.

The present study will not attempt a biographical treatment of Agee's life, although such a study would be illuminating, nor will it make a full-scale investigation of the relationship between Agee's work and the literary climate; that, too, would be illuminating, but is a work for the literary historian. The following pages will focus on the works themselves, with particular attention given to the aesthetic problems confronting Agee in his absolute commitment to the holiness of human reality.

Nor does this work aim at completeness. No effort has been made to study and discuss all the unpublished material. Even certain published items have been left unnoticed or mentioned only in passing. One reason, of course, is that such a complete study would, at the present stage, be excessively and prematurely extensive and also primarily descriptive. If the future grants to Agee his deserved reputation as one of the most original and meaningful talents of twentieth-century American literature, the field will be open for many additional and more detailed studies.

Instead, it has been my ambition to correct the common over-all image of Agee as a failure and an oddity in American letters or, obversely, as a victim to the forces of American culture, and to show his published works as they are in themselves. Out of Agee's work and life there springs forth, above all, a strong and enduring love—of God, of all things living or not living, of the universe as it is. I have considered it my duty and privilege, as scholar, critic, and human being, to honor and respond to that love.

It is a pleasure to acknowledge here the encouragement and assistance given me, directly and indirectly, by many friends and teachers at the University of New Mexico, in particular by Professors E. W. Tedlock, Jr., George Arms, Franklin M. Dickey, and Morris Freedman.

Montreal

P. O.

INTRODUCTION

*The road of excess leads to the
palace of wisdom.*
William Blake

Perhaps the best way to summarize the unique character
of James Agee's literary career is to say that it was, above
all, unfashionable and in constant conflict with what the
times demanded. Born in 1909 in Knoxville, Tennessee,
he managed to find fault with all the movements that have
shaped so much of twentieth-century art, politics, and
life. As a result, he seemed to produce very little of significance compared with those authors who embraced new
movements and took their places in the vanguard of more
or less popular opinions. In 1949, at the age of forty, he
had produced one book of poems, *Permit Me Voyage*
(1934); one long, sprawling prose work, *Let Us Now
Praise Famous Men* (1941), and innumerable articles in
Time, Fortune, and *The Nation.* Though his talents were
generally recognized, these works refused to fit any of
the convenient categories of established contemporary
writing and, consequently, were regarded more as indica-
tions of future masterpieces than as achievements in their
own right. As Dwight Macdonald has pointed out, Agee

"was always moderate in an immoderate way, he was always out of step, and he had very little respect for the *Zeitgeist.*" [1]

When Agee died in 1955, his reputation underwent a rapid metamorphosis. His novel, *A Death in the Family*, was published in 1957 and received the Pulitzer Prize posthumously. This sudden and belated recognition caused a flood of material to be released. Two volumes of *Agee on Film*, containing the film criticism and the film scripts, respectively, were edited and published in 1958 and 1960. In 1960, also, *Let Us Now Praise Famous Men* was re-issued and, although critics still found it difficult to cope with, it was promptly chosen, like all of the posthumous volumes, for most of the fashionable book clubs. *The Letters of James Agee to Father Flye* appeared in 1962 and was re-issued the following year in paperback form. And at the time of this writing, there is still more coming: two recently discovered chapters for *A Death in the Family*, discarded sections from *Let Us Now Praise Famous Men*, more letters, the poetry, together with hitherto unedited and uncollected poems in a new edition, a biography, four of his uncollected short stories from the *Harvard Advocate*.[2] And since Agee wrote prodigiously all his life, this list is probably by no means exhaustive.

The reasons for the reversal of the critical awareness of Agee are complex. Only a few of them will be suggested here. First of all, Agee's death at forty-five immediately evoked the image of the young genius cruelly brought

[1] Dwight Macdonald, *Against the American Grain* (New York: Random House, 1962), p. 164.

[2] Richard Culahan, "A Cult Grew Around a Many-Sided Writer," *Life,* LV (November 1, 1963), 72.

to an end before his prime. Macdonald even compares him with Keats in this respect and makes the difference in age a sociological fact: "that Keats was twenty-five and Agee forty-five doesn't alter the point. Agee was an American, of a race that matures slowly, if ever." [3] Secondly, Agee's career seemed a spectacular waste of talent, and as such it seemed to denounce in certain ways the American way of life. Instead of writing the great American novel, Agee spent sixteen years writing impeccable prose for the Luce empire, first on *Fortune* and later on *Time*, and this, in itself, is an arresting image of the predicament for the creative imagination in contemporary America. Thirdly, Agee's ability to survive, and preserve his integrity, in the world of journalism and, later, in Hollywood, became a testimony to the possibility of being a nonconformist in a conformist age and society; and in the late fifties and sixties this has been a dominant concern of a good many intellectuals.[4]

In an age when *avant-garde* artists can move from obscurity to financially and culturally rewarding fame in a matter of weeks, Agee has become an enviable image of the artist's integrity in a hostile society, recent enough to be relevant to the contemporary situation, yet distant enough to be worthy of veneration without imposing too seriously demanding obligations. No wonder, then, that Agee has become almost a culture hero, whose life has more significance than his work. Finally, what all this may add up to is a realization of guilt on the part of American intellectuals, an awareness that during his life-

[3] Macdonald, p. 159.
[4] *Vide* the works of David Riesmann *et al.*

time Agee did not receive the kind of support from them that he deserved, and that in this sense, therefore, the twentieth century has shown itself to be no more enlightened than previous centuries.

Although this sudden reversal of one man's literary reputation is interesting as a demonstration of the fickleness of the public literary mind, there is more than this to be learned from Agee's literary career. For Agee's work may serve to illuminate, by contrast, a good many of the preoccupations of twentieth-century American literature. In 1934, for instance, Agee published a collection of poems, *Permit Me Voyage*. The title was taken from a poem by Hart Crane, and the collection as a whole showed the considerable influence of Whitman, neither one of whom was accepted as a literary model after the thirties. Furthermore, the poetry was basically romantic and conventional in form at a time when everybody was experimenting with the breaking down of poetic form.

At a time when science was asserting itself most strongly, even in the field of psychology, Agee displayed a distinctly anti-scientific attitude, suggesting that scientific truth was only a partial truth and true only so far as it existed in the realm of "Truth" which he had the courage to assert as an absolute. And, finally, at the time when Eliot's Anglo-Catholicism was becoming fashionable, Agee's religiosity was at once more skeptical and more deeply felt and asserted itself more seriously as a matter of life and death rather than, as in Eliot's case, a matter of intellectual and poetic necessity. (Similarly, when in the late forties religious trends became so noticeable that *Partisan Review* felt called upon to organize a symposium on "Religion and the Intellectuals," Agee began his contribution by pointing out his "pro-religious" attitude, but immediately went on to say that he was "not on the whole delighted by this so-called revival." [5])

In much the same way, *Let Us Now Praise Famous Men* exists as a telling contrast to the prevailing literary climate in the late thirties and early forties. The work was undertaken, together with the photographer Walker Evans, as a documentary assignment for *Fortune* but ended, as Alfred Kazin has pointed out, "by being an attack on the facile mechanics and passivity of most documentary assignments." [6] While it was "fashionable" during the late thirties to be concerned over the sharecropping situation (much as it is now fashionable to be concerned over integration and poverty), Agee refused to see the problem in the facile terms of contemporary politics or sociology but tried to approach it, individualistically and rebelliously, simply as a human being. With typical sarcasm, he stated at the outset that together with Evans, he tried to deal with the subject "not as journalists, sociologists, politicians, entertainers, humanitarians, priests, or artists, but seriously." [7]

When *Let Us Now Praise Famous Men* was published in 1941, five years after it was begun, the sharecropping problem was no longer in fashion, but even if it had been and even if the war had not then been only a few months away, it is debatable whether the book could have gained appreciation as anything more than "the most distinguished failure of the season," [8] as *Time* called it. The book at-

[5] "Religion and the Intellectuals," *Partisan Review* XVII (February, 1950), 106–13.

[6] Alfred Kazin, *On Native Grounds* (New York: Reynal and Hitchcock, 1942), p. 495n.

[7] James Agee, *Let Us Now Praise Famous Men* (Boston: Houghton Mifflin Company, 1960), p. xv.

[8] Review of *Let Us Now Praise Famous Men, Time,* XXXVIII (October 13, 1941), 104.

tacked not only certain inhuman social conditions but also a good many of those intellectuals who might have been expected to sympathize with the ambition of Agee's exposé: while it was an implicit indictment of the politics of the Southern landowners, it also sneered at the naïveté, the misconceptions, the ignorance, and the humiliating compromises of New Deal reformers. And although he called himself a "Communist by sympathy and conviction," he also insisted on pointing out that Communism "is only a part of much more and a means to an end: and in every concession to a means, the end is put in danger of all but certain death." [9] In answer to an inquiry about his allegiance in case of war, Agee questioned, in the fall of 1940, "whether an individual can in good conscience serve, or register, by any requirement other than his own," [10] In an age which provided an abundance of political as well as aesthetic "movements" and saw the placing of allegiance as meritorious conduct, Agee's religiously observed individualism must have appeared oddly removed from all the contemporary trends.

Agee's film criticism, too, goes against the grain. While most criticism during the forties was either passionately concerned with the conventional aesthetics of the medium or else condescendingly aware of its literary possibilities, Agee insisted on seeing each movie as a totality which set up its own limitations and in which a simple sense of reality, of how the everyday world looks and exists, could outweigh the most elaborately and skillfully handled artifices. This willingness to accept and honor the real, wherever encountered, made him examine with equal care horror movies and classical dramas, silent comedies and

[9] *Let Us Now Praise Famous Men*, p. 356.
[10] *Ibid.*, p. 357.

escapist melodramas. This passion for reality is also evident
in his film scripts, which go to exaggerated length in indicating sequences, camera angles, and exact visual details.
They are, as Dwight Macdonald has put it, "the scripts of
a frustrated director," [11] and it is typical that Agee, disregarding the established fact that the director finally makes
his own film with very little help from the scriptwriter,
never could write an entirely conventional script but insisted on giving it all his talents.

Finally, the posthumous publication of *A Death in the
Family* brought Agee's mistimed career to its climax. For
although it received the Pulitzer Prize and its prose was
praised in glowing terms, many critics found it impossible
to judge adequately a work which was never finished by its
author and, furthermore, wondered whether it really was a
novel at all.[12] It seems only appropriate that this book,
which derives ultimately from Whitman and the romantics
in its method and sensibility, should have been published
at a time when critical opinion found it difficult to accept
Whitman as a model and demanded in literature order,
unity of themes, imagery, character and action, and structure. This literary climate was hardly conducive to the
appreciative reception of a work which is in itself a
fragment and which shirks structure in favor of "texture."

The question raised by James Agee's literary career is
not why he failed to conform to the trends of twentieth-
century American literature and culture, but why all those
movements which have embraced so many off-beat phenomena failed to see Agee's talent for what it was. In one
sense, Agee was himself responsible for this; to him the role

[11] Macdonald, p. 154.
[12] Cf. Leslie Fiedler, "Encounter with Death," *New Republic*,
CXXXVII (December 9, 1957), 25–26.

as outcast and rebel was identical to that as artist: "Every fury on earth has been absorbed in time, as art, or as religion, or as authority in one form or another. . . . Official acceptance is the one unmistakable symptom that salvation is beaten again . . . and is the kiss of Judas." [13]

But in a deeper sense, the failure to recognize Agee's existence as a major talent (disregarding now the matter of acceptance) indicates the predominance in twentieth-century America of dogmatic movements, in politics, in religion, in art. Communism, Catholicism, Social Realism, and later, the War Effort, and the positions of the Cold War, these and others have been ideological positions adopted with such rigidity that they distorted simple human reality. Agee was well aware of this situation, and even though it made most of his efforts into failures, he continued to write against that grain. Just as he advises the reader of *Let Us Now Praise Famous Men* to "bear the nominal subject, and his expectation of its proper treatment, steadily in mind," [14] so all his other works can be seen as a conscious effort to restore to human reality some of that dignity which he found bartered, stolen, or distorted by fashionable positions.

For example, in the remarkable early prose poem "Dedication," Agee tried to fuse his Anglo-Catholic experience of the world with an essentially "bardic" aesthetic ultimately derived from Whitman and demanding a radical subjectivity [15] in order to project an image of the world as real rather than as fiction. This awareness of the conflict between art and life is extended in *Let Us Now Praise*

[13] *Let Us Now Praise Famous Men*, p. 15.
[14] *Ibid.,* p. xv.
[15] Cf.·Walt Whitman's use of the phrase "I, Walt Whitman" in *Leaves of Grass.*

Famous Men, in which Agee tried to confront, as squarely as possible, the fact that the people he is writing about are, *a priori,* real, alive, human beings. This led to a realization that any book would be a falsification of their reality and that the only adequate response must avoid the suspension of disbelief which necessarily occurs with the reader's awareness that a book is *made.* In a manner similar to that of modern action painting, Agee tried to make his book the record of an event rather than the imitation of one; while the nominal subject is sharecropping, the real or actual subject is simply one human being's response not to an abstract problem but to the living reality of certain specified human beings. Despite the common notion that the book lacks organization, there is, in fact, a carefully outlined structure, which, however, is meaningfully only if the book is understood to be, not simply a report on certain social maladies, but "an effort in human actuality," [16] in which the reader's response is no different from what it would be in an actual human situation.

The conviction that human reality deserves above all a response in human and subjective rather than critical and objective terms also underlies Agee's film criticism. Agee's subjective and impressionistic method of discussing movies can, in effect, be seen as the result of a deliberate attitude: since to him the common distinction between art and life was artificial, any encounter with human reality, in fiction or in life, demanded a human response, and the constant presence of Agee as writer in the movie reviews was one way of asserting this belief. To Agee, however, this did not imply a narrow-minded insistence on realism at all costs; on the contrary, as the following pages will try to show in greater detail, his respect for human reality in all

[16] *Let Us Now Praise Famous Men,* p. xvi.

its forms made him realize all the more acutely the various contexts within which human events assume their meaning. Nor did it create an exaggerated preference for documentaries. The kind of film he looked forward to was fiction with courage and respect enough to let the poetry of the real world shine forth without disturbing it with cinematic artifice. To a certain extent, he set this goal for his own scripts, although he often appears to have been caught in the conflict between his love for the medium and the minor role played by the scriptwriter in the making of a movie. Though it is therefore impossible to judge the scripts as finished works of art, they show clearly that Agee was passionately involved in the medium and that he tried to live up to the ambition of fiction in collaboration with reality, which he demanded in his criticism.

In much the same way, Agee's fiction is concerned with the distinction between the reality of a work of art and the reality of life itself. Deriving its basic aesthetic from Whitman, *A Death in the Family* creates a tension between the chaotic nature of the experience involved and the poet's way of writing about it. Realizing, as in *Let Us Now Praise Famous Men*, that "words cannot embody; they can only describe," [17] the poet is faced with the recognition that his desire to recapture the original experience in its totality—and that desire is evident throughout the book—can never be satisfied; all he can do is to project meaning and order into the original chaos by means of his language. This changes the nature of the experience itself, and the meaning of the novel is not to be found in the behavior of such novelistic characters as Rufus or Mary Follet but in the writer's perception of them. In that sense, there is no distinction between a "real" and a fictional

[17] *Let Us Now Praise Famous Men*, p. 238.

world; what matters is the human response to *any* experience. The effort at comprehending the reality of death which is undertaken in the book, by the characters as well as by the author, fails to give any kind of meaningful result; the only thing that can be done is to affirm and to "celebrate" the mystery of life itself. This kind of celebration does not depend on the distinction between art and life. It is a simple human emotion, and, as such, it makes the novel itself more of a realization than a description of a certain reality.

This absolute commitment to the holiness of human reality is, then, the theme that runs through all of Agee's writing, and the following pages will examine it at greater length in order to determine if it is necessary to see Agee's career as a continuous waste of superior talent, or even, as W. M. Frohock has suggested, as the scattering of energy which will necessarily occur as long as American life invites creative talent in widely dispersed fields.[18] In one way, what follows is a simple justification of that career, an effort to show that, whatever the waste, the achievements themselves are considerable and impressive, and that there is no reason to deplore his wasted life any more than that of any other writer's.

[18] W. M. Frohock, "James Agee—The Question of Wasted Talent," in *The Novel of Violence in America* (Dallas: Southern Methodist University Press, 1957), pp. 212–230.

HONEST AND LOVELY
AND A LITTLE CLEAR

POETRY

Everybody seems to agree about Agee's poetic talents: the blurb writers assert that "Agee was essentially a poet"; John Huston, introducing Agee's scripts, writes that "in a sense it was all poetry"; [1] and Dwight Macdonald, a close friend and serious critic, pays tribute to the book jackets and points out that *A Death in the Family* is "really not a novel but a long poem on themes from childhood and family life." [2] In view of this agreement, it is somewhat surprising, at first, that Agee's poetic achievement is not greater than it is. He wrote poetry all his life: at Phillips Exeter Academy, at Harvard; and after he had published his only collection of poems, *Permit Me Voyage*, in 1934, he published poems in *Partisan Review*, in *Harper's Monthly*, in *Forum*. On the basis of the one poem he could have read at the time, Alfred Kreymborg mentioned Agee in *Our Singing Strength*, in 1929, (and, as Wilbur M. Frohock points out in *The Novel of Violence in America*, rather falsely assumed an influence from

Eliot [3]), and Louis Untermeyer later included Agee in his anthology *Modern American Poetry*; yet nobody seems to be willing to claim that Agee is even a minor poet of the twentieth century. While mentioning his poetry, most critics seem to prefer to go on to talk about the great lyrical qualities of Agee's novels, his screenplays, and his remarkable book about Southern sharecroppers.

Just before he entered Harvard, he showed his poetry to S. Foster Damon and to Robert Frost and received encouragement from them; [4] later, at Harvard, I. A. Richards told him his poetry was good.[5] Archibald MacLeish, in his foreword to *Permit Me Voyage*, found much to praise:

. . . a technical apprenticeship successfully passed, a mature and in some cases masterly control of rhythms, a vocabulary at once personal to the poet and appropriate to the intention and, above everything else, the one poetic gift which no amount of application can purchase and which no amount of ingenuity can fake—a delicate and perceptive ear.[6]

While the reviewers seemed to appreciate just that skill which MacLeish pointed to, they seemed less interested in what Agee had to say. E. L. Walton, for instance, wrote:

Mr. Agee's delight has been in literature. He has no simple and direct view of a real scene, no sensuous world of experience save books. He is so very excellent in what he has accomplished that we cannot but regret that his is not the new vision, that he sees so little, feels so little freshly.[7]

The *New York Times* reviewer, "C. G. P.," resorted mostly to critical platitudes:

Agee is a new poet with a fine, skillful talent. In his lines there is awareness of the changing ideas of society that are stirring the world. There is also a stubborn faith in enduring values.[8]

William Rose Benét's praise was mild and meaningless:

A new poet who is above the average and well worth your reading. I do believe that the perceptive ear for poetry is present in Agee.[9]

While praising Agee's long prose poem, "Dedication," David McCord found that "Mr. Agee's poetry is much concerned with love and Carew; and, as is so often the case with younger poets, the brief ideas are the best." [10] An exception to these rather bland judgments was the review by Lincoln Kirstein, who, as editor of *Hound and Horn*, had published Agee's long poem "Ann Garner" in 1928. Kirstein found that "except that Agee's constructed and choric forms include in their really singable lyricism a large quality of tragic strength, they apply in essence as much to present catastrophes as Blake's innocent songs did to his century." [11]

One can, of course, only suggest some reasons for this bland reception of Agee's poetry, as well as for the continuous lack of strong interest in it well after nearly all of his other works have been praised as masterpieces. MacLeish suggested one reason already in 1934, when he pointed to the untimely character of the poetry (untimeliness, incidentally, was to plague Agee all through his life): "It will not excite the new-generationers, left wing or right. Agee does not assume what is usefully known as a Position." [12] To find, in 1934, in a book of poems, not only "A Chorale" but also a cycle of twenty-five sonnets, an eight-page "Epithalamium," and an equally lengthy "Dedication" ("In much humility / to God in the highest / in the trust that he despises nothing"), mixing an almost Whitmanesque catalogue-technique with seventeenth-century Anglo-Catholicism, must have confused a considerable number of readers used to either Eliot's fashionable and anti-social spiritual agonies or Auden's sophisticated engagement in social issues.

Another reason is suggested by the extraordinary scope of Agee's ambition as he states it in his letters to Father Flye. In 1928, he comments on "Ann Garner":

Of course, a good deal of it is simply iambic prose—but I wrote that as a clothes-line on which to string my lyrics. It's funny—I can't write real lyrics—*subjective* things. I have to trump up a situation and story—and write them as of another character.[13]

But two years later, in November 1930, he outlines to Father Flye a poetic program in which the almost presumptuous ambition is matched by an amazing awareness of what is really at stake (even more so when one considers that he was at this time barely twenty-one years old). The letter must be quoted extensively:

I've got to make my mind as broad and deep and rich as possible, as quick and fluent as possible; abnormally sympathetic and yet perfectly balanced. At the same time, I've got to strengthen those segments of my talent which are naturally weak; and must work out for myself a way of expressing what I want to write. You see, I should like to parallel, foolish as it sounds, what Shakespeare did. That is, in general—to write primarily about people—giving their emotions and dramas the expression that because of its beauty and power, will be most likely to last. But—worse than that: I'd like, in a sense, to combine what Chekhov did with what Shakespeare did—that is, to move from the dim, rather eventless beauty of C. to huge geometric plots such as Lear. And to make this transition without its seeming ridiculous. And to do the whole so that it flows naturally, and yet, so that the whole—words, emotion, characters, situation, etc.—has a discernible symmetry and a very definite *musical* quality—inaccurately speaking—I want to *write symphonies.* That is, characters introduced quietly (as are themes in a symphony, say) will recur in new lights, with new verbal orchestration, will work into counterpoint and get a sort of monstrous grinding beauty—and so on. By now you probably see what I mean at least as well as I do.

Well—this can't be done to best advantage in a novel. Prose holds you down from the possibility of such music. And put into poetic drama, it would certainly be stillborn or worse; besides, much of what I want to get can't well be expressed in dialogue. It's got to be narrative poetry, but a sort that so far as I know has never been tried. In the sort I've read, the medium is too stiff to allow you to get exactly a finely shaded atmosphere, for instance—in brief, to get the effects that *can* be got in a short story or novel. I've thought of inventing a sort of amphibious style—prose that would run into poetry when the occasion demanded poetic expression. That may be the solution; but I don't entirely like the idea. What I want to do is, to devise a poetic diction that will cover the whole range of events as perfectly and evenly as skin covers every organ, vital as well as trivial, of the human body. And this style can't, of course, be incongruous, no matter what I'm writing about. For instance, I'm quite determined to include comedy in it—of a sort that would demand realist slangy dialogue and description.

That leads to another thing—the use of words in general. I'm very anxious not to fall into archaism or "literary" diction. I want my vocabulary to have a very large range, but the words *must* be alive.[14]

A year later, he indicates that he has been trying to carry out the program:

What writing I've done has been done almost rigidly as if I were composing music—not in accordance to definite musical form, but in intricacy of structure, recurrence of themes, and an attempt to write *impersonally*—the difference between pure music and program music. . . .[15]

Although he tried to put this program in effect in his poetry, that was not the right medium for it. The long prose poem "Dedication" is a noteworthy attempt, and traces of his ambition can be seen in the organization of the sonnet cycle, but it is in a short story from 1931, "They That Sow in Sorrow Shall Reap," [16] and, later, in *Let Us Now Praise Famous Men* that the program begins to bear fruit.

Nearly all of Agee's poems show a skillful handling of traditional forms: most of them are regularly stanzaic and employ rhymes in the traditional manner. The sonnets follow the Shakespearean pattern (ab ab cd cd ef ef gg), although they depend rather more heavily on the octave-sestet division than most of Shakespeare's. Occasionally, Agee tries alliterative exercises in the Hopkinsian manner, although the result is sometimes more obscure than lyric:

> Demure morning   morning margin
>   glows cold   flows foaled:
> Fouled is flown   float float   easily earth
>   before demurely
>
> Chance gems   leave their harbors
> Sparkle above leaves   whom light lifted.[17]

Along with the awareness of traditional forms went an awareness of traditional themes, which Agee sometimes used to make a comment in an ironical, historical perspec-

tive. This is obvious not only in "A Chorale" and "Epithalamium," the themes of which are almost given in the
titles (but given a more modern complexity by the poet),
but also in a pastiche such as "The Passionate Poet to His
Love":

> Come live with me and be my love
> Provided you think little of
> Such stodge encumbrances as friends
> Who keep their means for their own ends;
>
> Granted we mutually agree
> That yours was never a mother's knee,
> Or, if the spiteful slime should bud,
> Will nip the foetus while it's mud:
>
> Provided you can smoothly be
> Wife, mother and nonentity
> As metaphoric moods require;
> Provided also you admire
>
> Nor ever dare to criticize
> Each syllable that I devise,
> And shall apprise me (though I know it)
> Of my majority as a poet;
>
> And like four angels each with sword
> Will guard the Inception of the Word—
> If such persuasions aught can move
> Then live with me and be my love.[18]

The remarkable thing about this poem is that it uses the
model provided by Marlowe's original poem, not to poke
gentle fun at Marlowe, in the manner of so many pastiches,
but to provide an angry, ironic commentary on certain

modern attitudes. The original pastoral idyll of communion with (a slightly artificial) nature has here been provided with "such stodge encumbrances as friends / Who keep their means for their own ends"; instead of feeling secure in nature, the poet and his love agree that they, "if the spiteful slime should bud, / Will nip the foetus while it's mud," a rather extravagant flippancy, coming from a love poet. The poem moves up to the supreme blasphemy in suggesting that his mistress "like four angels each with sword / Will guard the Inception of the Word"—thus comparing himself without a hint of modesty to the Divine Creator—to come back to the seventeenth-century idiom which provides so ironic a commentary to what has been said: "If such persuasions aught can move, / Then live with me and be my love." Thus, the irony of the poem is provided by the fact that while the form or model used by the poet says one thing, the words themselves say another.

"The Passionate Poet to His Love" is not necessarily a remarkable poem, but it shows a clear awareness of the seventeenth-century model and employs a firm and clearly defined point of view with a mature handling of a basic type of ambiguity [19] to stress an angry irony. As a minor exercise, it is certainly remarkably effective. In another poem, the poet uses a traditional theme in a more straightforward manner:

> Child, should any pleasant boy
> Find you lovely, many could,
> Wind not up between your joy
> The sly delays of maidenhood:
>
> Spread all your beauty in his sight
> And do him kindness every way,

Since soon, too soon, the wolfer night
Climbs in between, and ends fair play. (II)*

This, of course, is an exercise on the old *carpe diem* theme,
and it is successful in its manner of combining lyrical grace
with modern conversational idiom ("every way," "the
wolfer night," "ends fair play," "climbs in between").
The subdued sexuality implicit in the images is, just as in
some seventeenth-century poetry, controlled by the grace
and ceremony of the presentation. But Agee has not made
an imitation; he has re-presented the theme in modern dress.

Another early poem shows an unusual approach to a
rather common theme, "Good Friday":

High in Dodona's swaying groves,
High in the grey, the glimmering oaks,
Dodona's cauldrons, convolute,
Groan on the wind strange prophecies.

Among the whispering laurel roves
Great Pan, and on the tall sky, smokes
Of Delphi write; and now are mute
The graded reeds of Pan: he sees

Across the grey, the glimmering seas,
A leafless tree take barren root
On Golgotha; he hears the strokes
Of iron on iron, and his own hooves

The iron strikes through. Against two trees
Are driven his outstretched hands. Strange fruit
Hangs in the grey, the glimmering oaks,
Hangs in Dodona's swaying groves.[20]

First of all, the rather unusual rhyming technique of repeating the four end-sounds given in the first stanza

* Page references refer, in this chapter, to *Permit Me Voyage* (New
Haven, Yale University Press, 1934)

through the next three stanzas is worth noticing. Secondly, the theme itself is traditional and one that intrigued the Renaissance and posed an artistic problem for writers such as Milton. With the coming of Christ, the pagan gods lost their divine function; instead of being the heroes or judges of classical tragedy, they became now, at most, precursors to the divine message of Christ. In Renaissance poetry, for instance, Pan appears as a symbol of Christ; and while this may seem anachronistic, it did solve the problem, for the Renaissance, of retaining the classical form while giving it a Christian character.

Agee handles the shift from Pan to Christ with a sure sense of ambiguity which makes the poem effective. The death of Christ on the cross, which Pan observes "across the grey, the glimmering seas," becomes the death of Pan himself, *his* crucifixion; and this death, in turn, becomes in the end a human sacrifice in "Dodona's swaying groves" (Dodona was the place of the oracle of Zeus in Epicurus, whose response was interpreted from the rustling of oak leaves). And yet, a human sacrifice is exactly what Christ is, and thus we return to the first sense of the crucifixion, in the same way that the first two lines of the poem, anaphoric in structure, are repeated with only slight modification as the final two lines.

Since the poem begins with the world of Pan, the imagery is classical rather than Christian: Agee even avoids mentioning the cross and calls it the "leafless tree" taking "barren root / on Golgotha." When the poem ends, "Dodona's swaying groves" of "the grey, the glimmering oaks" have been given a new meaning by the human sacrifice that we have witnessed, but this has been done without bringing in any of the details that we generally associate with the shift from pagan to Christian.

While this shift is handled in the poem with great skill, it is also worth noting that the poem derives its tone not from the ironies in the treatment, but from the absolute objectivity with which the scene is regarded. Agee here avoids all value judgments; the adjectives are descriptive rather than emotional. In this way, the abstract pattern of the Christian mystery of Good Friday is given concreteness through the objective tone as well as through the concreteness of the "classical" imagery. This is what makes the poem an impressive effort and saves it from the charge of being too "academic" in conception.

On the whole, it can be said that Agee's poetry, especially in *Permit Me Voyage*, exists in a field between two poles: one of them is the example of the sixteenth- and seventeenth-century Elizabethans, Donne, Shakespeare, and others; the other is provided by such American poets as Whitman and Hart Crane. Agee was of course familiar with the metaphysical poets; in his letters he writes: "I've been reading a good deal of John Donne and Herbert, Vaughan, and Emily Dickinson, whose work bears a remarkable resemblance to Donne." [21] And the preparation he foresees for himself in his long letter to Father Flye seems to recall Donne in its conjunction of opposites into balance: "I've got to make my mind as broad and deep and rich as possible, as quick and fluent as possible; abnormally sympathetic and yet perfectly balanced." [22] In certain sections of Agee's "Epithalamium," the use of paradox recalls Donne and the Elizabethans, even though Agee's language avoids the angularly strong lines of Donne:

> For that the flesh arises like a wall
> Between two souls, all love has known distress.

But they have conquered sorrow, conquered all
That clouded love: are one in nothingness.

Such nothingness remains, and yet is gone,
Looks upon all, and yet is void of sight,
Quickens the roots of every flowering dawn,
Coils in the core of every ripening night:

It breathes from steady water, is the pain
Of bursting seeds, the agony of earth
Shuddering out its life; . . .   (43)

In the "Sonnets," Agee sometimes employs the kind of
direct and forcefully conversational opening line that we
have learned to associate with Donne:

What curious thing is love that you and I
Hold it impervious to all distress
And insolent in gladness set it high
Above all other joy and goodliness?   (49)

Why am I here? Why do you look at me
Triumphantly and lovingly and long?   (50)

Is love then royal on some holy height?
Thence does he judge us, thence dispense his grace? (51)

Those former loves wherein our lives have run
Seeing them shining, following them far,
Were but a hot deflection of the sun,
The operation of a migrant star.   (55)

The sonnet cycle, in fact, reminds one of the Elizabethans in its meditational nature: all twenty-five sonnets

deal with the human condition conceived in Anglo-Catholic (or, for that matter, Catholic) terms. The first sonnet, significantly, begins with Adam and the world which he has left to mankind:

> So it begins. Adam is in his earth
> Tempted and fallen, and his doom made sure
> O, in the very instant of his birth:
> Whose deathly nature must all things endure.
> The hungers of his flesh, and mind, and heart
> That governed him when he was in the womb,
> These ravenings multiply in every part:
> And shall release him only to the tomb.
> Meantime he works the earth, and builds up nations,
> And trades, and wars, and learns, and worships chance,
> And looks to God, and weaves the generations
> Which shall his many hungerings advance
> When he is sunken dead among his sins.
> Adam is in his earth. So it begins.   (46)

This is the beginning, the origin, of the human condition. No image could better symbolize for Agee the plight of mankind than the picture of Adam, "his doom made sure / O, in the very instant of his birth," yet struggling against all odds to find for himself a release from those "hungers" which define his life. In its circular movement (the first line occurs with a slight reversal as the last line), the sonnet suggests, in fact, the history of all mankind, and this sense is supported by the sestet which rises above Adam's particular situation as a human individual to examine the life he has made for himself, with work, trades and wars, and to see him as the weaver of generations: here is our beginning in history.

With this situation in mind, the rest of the twenty-five sonnets explore the human condition in greater detail. The succeeding sonnet, for instance, begins: "Our doom is in our being. We began / In hunger eager more than ache of hell," and goes on to explore how this "hunger" dominates the human condition. This, of course, is Agee's conception of original sin, of man's predestined shortcomings, but it is significant that he chooses to call it hunger rather than desire. It is one of Agee's characteristics, all through his works, that he reduces such an absolute concept as the human condition to its most elemental terms: in that sense, "hunger" is more concrete than "desire," which has largely psychological connotations. Also, Agee was never blind to the human quality in this hunger, even though it stands as an opposite to the divine in man: in the sonnet, he continues with a set of paradoxes discussing just this:

> And in that hunger became each a man
> Ravened with hunger death alone may spell:
> And in that hunger live, as lived the dead,
> Who sought, as now we seek, in the same ways,
> Nobly, and hatefully, what angel's-bread
> Might ever stand us out these short few days. (46)

"Hunger" and "angel's-bread," "nobly, and hatefully," these are paradoxes that seem to define the human predicament.

The attempt to see the human situation in terms as elemental as possible leads Agee, in the third sonnet, to describe a human life in terms of the changing seasons, not, however, with the emphasis on how a human life can be said to correspond in its stages to the various seasons of spring, summer, fall, and winter, but with a wealth of

concrete details which emphasize and give richness to the
inevitability of their passing:

> The wide earth's orchard of your time of knowing,
> Shine of the springtime pleasures into bloom
> And branched throes of health; but soon the snowing
> And tender foretaste of your afterdoom,
> Of fallen blossoming air persuades the air
> In hardier practices: and soon dilate
> Fruits and the air together that shall bear
> Earthward the heavied boughs and to their fate. . . . (47)

In the fourth sonnet, the poet examines the human
condition from yet another point of view: looking back
on the line of his ancestors, he sees their valiant striving
as well as their failure, and realizes that the same strife
is now his, and that the knowledge of inevitable failure
does not excuse him from the task:

> I have been fashioned on a chain of flesh
> Whose backward length is broken on the dust:
> Frail though the dust and small as the dew's mesh
> The morning mars, it holds me to a trust:
> My flesh that was, long as this flesh knew life,
> Strove and was valiant, still strove, and was naught:
> Now it is mine to wage their valiant strife
> And failing seek still what they ever sought.
> I have been given strength they never wore.
> I have been given hope they never knew.
> And they were brave, who can be brave no more.
> And they that live are kind as they are few.
> 'Tis mine to touch with deathlessness their clay:
> And I shall fail, and join those I betray.   (47)

In one sense, this is a declaration of human fallibility as
proclaimed by Catholic dogma (Catholic rather than Prot-

estant because of the emphasis on "their valiant strife"
rather than on "faith"), but even more, it is a statement that
the inevitable failure is what gives dignity to and, in fact,
defines a human being, and that every new generation, with
its new strength and new hope, must define itself through
a new strife and a new failure. This is so not merely in
theological terms but also in all human activities: in sonnet
VIII and the following sonnets, the failure of love is
explored:

> Be mindful that all love is as the grass
> And all the goodliness of love the flower
> Of grass, for lo, its little day shall pass
> And withering and decay define its hour.   (49)

Finally, in the last sonnet of the cycle, the failure of the
poet himself is mentioned:

> These are confusing times and dazed with fate:
> Fear, easy faith, or wrath's on every voice:
> Those toward the truth with brain are blind or hate:
> The heart is cloven on a hidden choice:
> In which respect I still shall follow you.
> And when I fail, know where the fault is due.   (58)

"Failure," said Melville in his essay on Hawthorne, "is the
true test of greatness," and Agee is constantly concerned
with the quality of human failure (and, as will be shown
later, in *Let Us Now Praise Famous Men*, the artistic
problem becomes one of taking failure into account during
the creation of a work of art, to make the very failure
itself into art). Instead of turning this awareness of failure
into a gloomy righteousness over human depravity, Agee
sees it as what must be affirmed if one wants to be human:

AGEE.

This little time the breath and bulk of being
Are met in me: who from the eldest shade
Of all undreamt am raised forth into seeing
As I may see, the state of all things made:
In sense and dream and death to make my heart
Wise in the loveliness and natural health
Of all, and God, upon the void a part:
Likewise to celebrate this commonwealth:
Believing nothing, and believing all,
In love, in detestation, but most
In naught to sing of all: to recall
What wisdom was before I was this ghost:
Such songs I shall not make nor truths shall know:
And once more mindless into truth shall go.   (57)

To go "mindless into truth": that is not only to accept the "certain ill" (56) of sure failure but also to embrace it, in fact, to refuse to transcend the human situation. It means accepting being with the "breath and bulk of being" instead of assuming a perspective which is alien to human nature (although it may at times seem preferable). In essence, it is a decision to accept the self rather than to assume a self which is not; and in terms of the poet's own aesthetic struggle, this is what Agee affirms in the twenty-fourth sonnet:

Sure fortitude must disabuse my mind
Of all enlargements in unfounded hope
That I perceive whom fear of self made blind
My destiny constrained in my own scope.
All memory of magnificence of sound,
All grandeur and finality of words,
All nobleness some alien pain has found
That lives here painless, let them be interred.
Those men I worship and would stand among

In death well gained and reverently would greet,
Those immense souls have peopled mine too long,
And blown it broad with hope that was deceit:
And my poor soul, if aught it would create,
Must fast of these, and feed on its own fate. (57)

The fear of self can blind one to the reality of the self;
through reading, through imitation, through admiration, it
can people the soul with other souls that encourage a hope
that is closer to deceit because it does not derive from the
self. Therefore, the poet, if he hopes to create something,
must free himself, become himself, and rid himself of
remembered phrases and beautiful idioms, "memory of
magnificence of sound, / All grandeur and finality of
words," in order to "stand in hope to make myself a man"
(58). This search for a personal idiom is an acceptance
of a radical subjectivity, which for Agee has its basis both
in the human reality and in theological doctrine.[23] (Later,
of course, it is this kind of radical subjectivity which
underlies the working method of *Let Us Now Praise
Famous Men.*)

In human terms, what accompanies this acceptance is
love. For in love one recreates the discovery of the world:

And now, but slowly, see our hearts awake.
The eyes unshut, the living sight shine clear:
How still each heart reluctant lies to take
The image of its image: though so near
We lie, that surely both our hearts perceive
Identities they scarcely yet believe.   (54)

Having recovered, then, one's true identity, the world lies
open through love, and Agee celebrates this love in a
sonnet filled with images of a world which is just waking

up, or being rediscovered, at dawn. This is perhaps the best of the sonnets in the whole cycle, joining a delicate precision of language, alliteration ("the pure-leaved air dwells passionless as glass," "darkness loiters leaf to leaf releasing"), and assonance ("leaf releasing," "the morning's deep-drawn strength increasing / Till the sweet land . . . But sleeping still"), with a clear conception of purpose:

> Now stands our love on that still verge of day
> Where darkness loiters leaf to leaf releasing
> Lone tree to silvering tree: then slopes away
> Before the morning's deep-drawn strength increasing
> Till the sweet land lies burnished in the dawn:
> But sleeping still: nor stirs a thread of grass:
> Large on the low hill and the spangled lawn
> The pure-leaved air dwells passionless as glass:
> So stands our love new found and unaroused,
> Appareled in all peace and innocence,
> In all lost shadows of love past still drowsed
> Against foreknowledge of such imminence
> As now, with earth outshone and earth's wide air,
> Shows each to other as this morning's fair.   (55)

Even after this brief discussion of Agee's sonnets, it should be clear that the sonnets at least attempt what Agee meant when he said, "I want to *write symphonies.* That is, characters introduced quietly (as are themes in a symphony, say) will recur in new lights, with new verbal orchestration, will work into counterpoint and get a sort of monstrous grinding beauty...." [24] For while the theme of the whole cycle is the condition of man as defined by religious doctrine, it occurs with many subtle variations in new settings to throw new light on a different situation. This is perhaps the most noteworthy achievement of the cycle as a whole and it points up to what Agee was later to attempt. Considered separately, as poems, the individual sonnets are not always successful; in general, they suffer from their close approximation of seventeenth-century poetics and a slightly archaic style, but when they do succeed, as do sonnets XX, XXII, and XXIV, to cite only three, they have a clear precision of language, a delicate concreteness of imagery, and a subtle sense of rhythm.

Yvor Winters has called "A Chorale" a "remarkable poem" (without explaining why [25]), but perhaps the most remarkable thing about the poem is simply the effort to write "a chorale." The choice of genre is itself symptomatic of Agee's strong commitment to his religious background, and the poem struggles to find adequate expressions for this commitment in a world which has turned its back on it. Thus, the poem grows out of the poet's sense of religion as providing a standard for judgment, and it is the radical nature of the poet's choice which is perhaps more amazing than anything else. For it would seem that the poem remains too strongly bound by its own sense of archaism to be quite effective: instead of the awareness of tradition in a new dress (such as we can find it in, say, Eliot or Auden), the poem gives us an elegantly contrived pastiche.

While there are fine passages that are modern in the best sense of the word (such as "Great God kind God the deep fire-headed fountain / Of earth and funneled hell and hopeful mountain"), the diction in general, for instance, echoes the Book of Common Prayer (neologisms like "heartsearth" and "allsalvation" presumably modeled on words like "lovingkindness") or early Bible translations ("sweet earth," "wasting shadow," "sickly slow," "ghosted

Gods"). The syntax in the first few stanzas is so uncomfortable that it makes one think of Milton's worst Latinizing excesses. In this way, we get mainly imitation rather than original; and this failure to reconcile the tradition with the present can be seen in the following couplet (addressed to Christ):

> The time is withered of your ancient glory:
> Your doing in this sweet earth a pretty story. (37)

It seems safe to suggest that the words "a pretty story" are meant to be ironic in this context, yet they fail because the tone of flippancy they engender has not been logically or emotionally suggested in the earlier stanzas, where, on the contrary, the present evil state of the world is discussed in the loftiest rhetoric ("How knowledge muffles wisdom's eye to danger: / How greed misrules: how greed's enraged avenger / Swears greed the equal prize for man's pursuing, / And your undoing").

Despite this failure, however, it is the tone of the poem which attracts attention. The poet's attitude to his material reveals an uncompromising attempt to judge the deterioration of the modern world from certain basic values of the Christian tradition. The poem also shows clearly that the poet has realized the need for a rhetoric of some sort to lift the matter out of its everyday connections and make it "poetically" true. In other words, we find here Agee's realization that the conflict between the Christian tradition and the decay of the modern world cannot be resolved in realistic terms if it is not to turn into a trivial quarrel; the high rhetoric is needed to lift the poem to a level on which the conflict can be meaningfully resolved in the minds of the poet and his reader. Unfortunately, Agee's rhetoric borrows so much from the Elizabethans that the poem becomes little more than a pastiche; but the attempt is in itself worthy of notice for it foreshadows the kind of attack on a literary problem which appears in *Let Us Now Praise Famous Men*. Above all, there is evident in the poem passion as well as compassion, high seriousness, and humility:

> If this your Son is now indeed debasèd
> Among old effigies of God effacèd,
> Blaze in our hearts who still in earth commend you:
> Who through all desolation will defend you:
> For we are blinded all and steep are swervèd
> Far among many Deaths who still would be preservèd.

The same tone is present in the best poem of the collection. "Dedication" begins with the following words: "In much humility / to God in the highest / in the trust that he despises nothing" (16); and under the heading "And in his commonwealth," it goes on to list a long number of people, places, and things to whom the poet directs his dedication. Exactly what it is that the poet dedicates is not immediately clear: it may be his book of poems, or it may be his life, or it may be the spiritual effort of the person who happens to be writing the lines.

Essentially, the poem is based on the same conception that underlies "A Chorale": the world is seen in a traditional Anglo-Catholic manner with God as the inevitable point on which the structure of the world is based. The poet's emphasis, as he looks at the world, on continuous human failures, is, again, a reflection of the traditional Christian concept of human fallibility. But it is more than that; for the long dedication, which ends with a supplication for divine mercy, is not only directed to God, to his saints, to all great artists, truth-tellers and truth-knowers, but also to all those who have failed as well: to "those who died in deadly sin," to warmongers, to "those who think that any one man is wholly guilty," to "those who are more evil than kind." A dedication which is so directed in opposing directions seems, at first, almost to annihilate itself. But by embracing opposites (almost in the manner of Whitman's "I am large. I contain multitudes") the poet accepts the world in the moment of defining it. Opposites do not merely cancel each other: they are one way of defining the world; black and white may cancel each other but they define the world in terms of the spectrum. That Agee's poem is such a definition was perceptively noted by Lincoln Kirstein in his review, when he wrote: "In atmosphere it is a prayer, but it is also a cosmology . . . a comprehensive globelike symbol of the present, its accumulative past, its indicated future." [26]

The question then is: how does Agee define the world in his poem? First of all, he does it in terms of truth and those who seek the truth and tell it. After the introductory dedication to God, the poet begins a list of specific people:

. . . those who in all times have sought truth and who have told it in their art or in their living, who died in honor; and chiefly to these: Christ: Dante: Mozart: Shakespeare: Bach: Homer: Beethoven: Swift: the fathers of Holy Scripture: Shelley: Brahms: Rembrandt: Keats: Cézanne: Gluck: Schubert: Lawrence: Van Gogh and to an unknown sculptor of China, for his god's head.

To those of all times who have sought truth and who have failed to tell it in their art or in their lives, and who now are dead. (16)

This list is followed later by an enumeration of living truth-tellers:

To those living and soon to die who tell truth or tell of truth, or who honorably seek to tell, or who tell the truths of others: especially to James Joyce; to Charles Spencer Chaplin; to Ivor Armstrong Richards; to Archibald MacLeish; to William Butler Yeats; to Pablo Picasso; to Albert Edward Housman; to Stephen Spender; to Roy Harris; to Albert Einstein; to Frederick Burrhus Skinner; to Walker Evans; to Diego Rivera; to Orozco; to Ernest Hemingway; to Scott Fitzgerald; to Arturo Toscanini; to Yehudi Menuhin; to Irvine Frost Upham; to Robert Fitzgerald. (17–18)

Lists similar to these appear later in *Let Us Now Praise Famous Men*, and although they may seem to be merely enumerations of the author's likes or dislikes, they serve a more significant purpose. The overwhelming majority of the names are those of artists (and it is worth noting that Agee has included Chaplin among them), but there are also religious leaders, teachers (Richards), and scientists (Skinner and Einstein). In the lists, they become concrete examples of those who affirm truth, "in their art or in their living." For such a list to become effective, it has to be as varied as possible: it must affirm truth wherever it can be found. This means that it has to affirm life as well as art; it even has to affirm failure, for the value of truth is above success or failure (in the sense that we use these words commonly). Thus, Agee does not stop with these lists, but returns later to the truth of religion: "To those who know God lives, and who defend him" (18); and to the truth of scientists: "To all pure scientists, anatomists of truth and its revealers; in scorn of their truth as truth; and in thanksgiving for their truth in its residence in truth" (19). And in the same fashion, he affirms the truth of those people who simply live on earth:

To those who have built this time in the earth in all its ways and who dwell in it variously as they may or must: farmers

and workers and wandering men and builders and clerks and
legislators and priests and doctors and scientists and governors
of nations and engineers and prisoners and servants and sailors
and airmen and artists: in cities amassed, and on the wide
water, and lonesome in the air, and dark under the earth, and
laboring in the land, and in materials, and in the flesh, and in
the mind, and in the heart: knowing little and less of great
and little matters: enduring all things and most enduring living,
each in his way of patience . . . (22)

The total effect of all these lists is an assertion that truth
is meaningless as an abstract term and can only be comprehended as it is "lived," be it in the work of an artist or the
life of a farmer. In that sense, the life of any person is a
poem, just as any poem partaking of truth (be it even the
truth of a lie) exists in the real world, rather than as something made, something artificial.

In another sense, of course, these lists *are* indicative of
the author's subjective likes and dislikes: Agee even goes so
far as to include in his dedication his close family, relatives,
friends, and teachers, all mentioned by name. Yet this, it
would seem, is a result of the realization that in order to
define the world poetically a *radically subjective* point of
view is necessary. The way to avoid the charge of solipsism
or personal idiosyncrasy is not to affect a veneer of scientific objectivity, but to move deeper into the subjective
point of view as something given from the beginning, and
then to *act* within the field thus established. The world defined for us is uncontestably the poet's own world, but it is
saved from the incomprehensibility of private perception
because we have been given the private *person* of the poet
as something given, as the starting point outside of which
it is impossible even to approach the material.

This notion is interesting because it appears again, more

explicitly, as the working method of *Let Us Now Praise Famous Men*, and, also, because it is present in some of the writers in the American tradition Agee saw himself as belonging to. In two paragraphs in "Dedication," he writes:

To Mark Twain; to Walt Whitman; to Ring Lardner; to Hart Crane; to Abraham Lincoln; and to my land and to the squatters upon it and to their ways and words in love; and to my country in indifference.

To the guts and to the flexing heart and to the whole body of this language in much love, in grief for my dullness and in shame for my smallness and meagreness and caution. May I in time become so worthy of it as man may become of his words. (17)

The names mentioned here could all, to borrow Philip Rahv's famous distinction, be classified as "redskins" rather than "palefaces": they belong to a distinctly American tradition, closely related to the pioneers, the conquest of the West, and the native American idiom in language. Most interesting, perhaps, is his acknowledgment of Whitman. Already in 1927 he had written to Father Flye about *Leaves of Grass*:

I've been reading *Leaves of Grass* since I came back. You know, since last winter or so I've been feeling something—a sort of universal—oh, I don't know, feeling the beauty of everything, not excluding slop-jars and foetuses—and a feeling of love for everything—and now I've run into Walt Whitman —and it seems as if I'd dived into a sort of infinitude of beautiful stuff—all the better (for me) because it was just what has been knocking at me unawares.[27]

But such "a feeling of love for everything" leads easily (and dangerously) into the kind of romantic disorder of which Whitman has so often been (falsely) accused; and Agee seems to have learned from Whitman how to control it, how to make it part of the poetic process, how, in effect, to enact it within the poem itself. R. W. B. Lewis has given a pertinent description of how this aesthetic operates in Whitman's poetry:

For if the hero of *Leaves of Grass* radiates a kind of primal innocence in an innocent world, it was not only because he had made that world, it was also because he had begun by making himself. . . . What is implicit in every line of Whitman is the belief that the poet *projects* a world of order and meaning and identity into either a chaos or a sheer vacuum; he does not *discover* it. The poet may salute the chaos; but he creates the world.[28]

This is an essentially dynamic process, and in this it is different from what we mean when we say that every poet creates his own world. To Whitman, the poem is *literally* the world, rather than as in most poets the selective embodiment of an already existing world.[29] Therefore, the poem does not refer to an act of perception, but constitutes in itself that perception: "instead of describing reality, a poem is a realization," as Charles Fiedelson puts it.[30] The identity of the poet is crucial here, for in a very real sense he is his own world: "the 'I' of Whitman's poems speaks the world that he sees, and sees the world that he speaks, and does this by *becoming* the reality of his vision and of his words, in which the reader also participates." [31] In the same way, in Agee, the poet's radical subjectivity in defining himself *becomes*, in effect, a definition of the world.

This kind of aesthetics implies in itself an attitude toward language, as R. W. B. Lewis has pointed out:

. . . the process of naming is for Whitman nothing less than the process of creation. This new Adam is both maker and namer; his innocent pleasure, untouched by humility, is colored by the pride of one who looks on his work and finds it good. The things that are named seem to spring into being at the sound of the word.[32]

Whitman himself, in *An American Primer*, suggested that "*Names* are magic: One word can pour such a flood through the soul," [33] and Feidelson has commented that "since Whitman regards meaning as an activity of words rather than an external significance attached to them, language, together with the self and the material world, turns out to be a process, the pouring of the flood." [34] No wonder then that Whitman could claim that "the United States themselves are essentially the greatest poem." [35] For the practical purpose of the poet, there is no more a distinction between word and thing than there is between art and life, and the enumeration of things in those endless catalogues or lists (in both Whitman and Agee) is, as Feidelson suggests, "actually a process in which the known world comes into being." [36] Thus, Whitman suggests the criteria for style as he sees it; and they turn, of course, into still another catalogue:

Latent, in a great user of words, must actually be all passions, crimes, trades, animals, stars, God, sex, the past, might, space, metals, and the like—because these are the words, and he who is not these, plays with a foreign tongue, turning helplessly to dictionaries and authorities.[37]

These criteria can conveniently be compared with Agee's discussion of style in a letter to Father Flye:

I've thought of inventing a sort of amphibious style—prose that would run into poetry when the occasion demanded poetic expression. That may be the solution; but I don't entirely like the idea. What I want to do is, to devise a poetic diction that will cover the whole range of events as perfectly and evenly as skin covers every organ, vital as well as trivial, of the human body.[38]

It is this ambition which, in "Dedication," underlies his tribute "to the guts and to the flexing heart and to the whole body of this language in much love" as well as the linking of Mark Twain and Ring Lardner with Walt Whitman. In fact, in a review in the *Harvard Advocate*, in May 1931, Agee discussed the serious use of the American idiom in literature, mentioning Dashiell Hammett, Sherwood Anderson, and Ernest Hemingway, and considering Ring Lardner as a great master of style with a slightly limited subject matter.[39] Typically, too, both Agee and Whitman conceive of their poetic work in metaphors of the body and of musical composition, Agee in passages quoted above, and Whitman, for instance, in his famous statement that "my poems, when complete should be a *unity*, in the same sense that the earth is, or that the human body (senses, soul, head, trunk, feet, blood, viscera, man-root, eyes, hair) or that a perfect musical composition is." [40]

In "Dedication," Agee has hardly been able to realize his ambition; that was to come later. But he seems to have felt that if he wanted to write truthfully about his experiences as a twentieth-century American, Whitman would have to be one of his models, and that this could be done through the process of discovering the self and the world in language. Whitman, however, structured his seemingly sprawling poems around the idea of America and the

American experience in order to create, as James E. Miller has suggested, an American epic.[41] That kind of structure needed space, more space than Agee could afford in a short poem. But the device of making his poem a "dedication" or a prayer serves the same purpose, for it anchors the poem structurally outside of its own matter,[42] outside time and space, in God, so as to make the matter of the poem a creative discovery which, in terms of the poem itself, may be objectively accepted by the reader. It is from this point of view that "Dedication" must be seen as a religious poem. It does not deal with religious emotion as such, but it assumes a religious world picture, and in creating that world, its aesthetic makes, in effect, an analogy between the divine creation of the world and the artistic process.[43] Furthermore, in trying to embrace contradictions, to accept the human predicament in whatever its forms, the artist grants to the world itself that freedom which in traditional Christianity is the keynote of God's creation of the world.

If "Dedication" is a remarkable poem, it is because Agee, through the influence of Walt Whitman, has been able to fuse the two elements of his material, his Anglo-Catholic tradition and his realization of the basic uniqueness of the individual experience. The Whitman influence remains, in modified forms, in other works of his career; and in a later poem such as "Sunday: Outskirts of Knoxville, Tenn." it has been molded into a tender perception of the cosmic perspective on a precisely observed situation in a Southern small town. The poem opens with a gentle and delicate spring scene, in which, as Elizabeth Drew has pointed out,[44] the lyrical mood is stressed by the sound pattern, by end rhymes, and by alliteration:

> There, in the earliest and chary spring, the dogwood
> flowers.

Unharnessed in the friendly sunday air
By the red brambles, on the river bluffs,
Clerks and their choices pair.

Thrive by, not near, masked all away by shrub and
    juniper
The ford v eight, racing the chevrolet.

They cannot trouble her:

Her breasts, helped open from the afforded lace,
Lie like a peaceful lake,
And on his mouth she breaks her gentleness:

Oh, wave them awake!

This idyllic scene is followed by a meditative passage in
which the lyrical mood assumes a graver, more objective
tone:

They are not of the birds. Such innocence
Brings us to break us only.
Theirs are not happy words.

We that are human cannot hope.
Our tenderest joys oblige us most.
No chain so cuts the bone; and sweetest silk most
    shrewdly strangles.

After this observation on the basic instability of human
happiness follows a long Whitmanesque catalogue of
things to come, an almost cinematic vision of the dreary
terms of human existence:

How this must end, that now please love were ended,
In kitchens, bedfights, silences, women's pages,
Sickness of heart before goldlettered doors,

Stale flesh, hard collars, agony in antiseptic
    corridors,
Spankings, remonstrances, fishing trips, orange juice,
Policies, incapacities, a chevrolet,
Scorn of their children, kind contempt exchanged,
Recalls, tears, second honeymoons, pity,
Shouted corrections of missed syllables,
Hot water bags, gallstones, falls downstairs,
Oldfashioned christmases, suspicions of theft,
Arrangements with morticians taken care of by sons
    in law,
Small rooms beneath the gables of brick bungalow,
The tumbler smashed, the glance between daughter
    and husband,
The empty body in the lonely bed
And, in the empty concrete porch, blown ash
Grandchildren wandering the betraying sun

Now, on the winsome crumbling shelves of the horror
God show, God blind these children.[45]

This poem is, in many ways, typical of Agee at his best. Its tone, for instance, moves from the gentle idyll to a somber meditation to a furious vision and concludes with compassionate prayer. The imagery in the first section is unified by its common derivation from nature and provides a natural contrast with the jumbled images of the last section. The image of the woman with her breasts "like a peaceful lake," breaking "her gentleness" on the mouth of her lover serves as a preparation for the final image of helpless children: "God show, God blind these children." [46]

Perhaps the most impressive thing about Agee, as poet or as writer generally, is his ability to see any situation in the most elementary terms in order to project more clearly its human implications. In the early poetry, his use of nature imagery and his use of the seasons as images of human situations serve this purpose. This is evident also in the early blank-verse poem "Ann Garner" (written in 1928, and later reprinted in *Permit Me Voyage*). In a letter to Father Flye, quoted earlier, he called it "simply iambic prose" written as "a clothes-line on which to string my lyrics." [47] The remark is somewhat curious in view of the fact that only about one-tenth of the poem consists of genuinely lyrical passages—but then Agee's blank verse is often impressively poetic and quite removed from "iambic prose."

The story is strongly suffused with elements of folklore and myth. A farm woman bears a stillborn child, and this becomes almost a pact between her and nature, which the poet puts into the following incantation:

> Let him live in womb and womb of earth;
> In the swelling seed of every plant
> Let him live.
> Let him distill on rising mists,
> Let him be blown along the sky,
> Let him rise through womb and womb of light;
> With stars at their birth
> Let him again be born.   (25)

This fusion of sexual and nature imagery, which makes Ann almost a nature goddess, is heightened even more in the section where she sees nature come alive one night in spring; to her, of course, this is the rebirth of her child:

> . . . From field and forest life welled upward,
> And from the sky life fell like streaming rain
> And lay upon the earth in a black flood.

Over the rock-rimmed pasture heights, the stars
Poured through the sky, and earthward from the sky
Struck silver rods of starlight, in black prisms
Of night.
        Ann stood a moment, hands upraised,
Then sank upon the grave, her body tense
Against the earth. And there she lay until
Dawn's white sun-bladed wings soared up the east.
Then standing up, beneath her feet she saw
Fields rear their arched brown backs above the mists,
Saw the wild foaming green on every tree.
She saw black cattle moving through the dawn
Up heights of pasture. Through the spreading dawn
Leaped a wild, silver wind, that circled round her,
Then gathered all its power and blew against
And through her, whipping her joy-maddened body
Into the riot and revel of its dance.   (28)

This, obviously, is not the elegant blank verse of Eliot, with echoes of Laforgue and the Elizabethans; rather, in its narrative character as well as in its careful attention to the rural milieu it reminds one of Robert Frost. But there is a fury and an extravagance in the imagery which surpass the measured balance of Frost's manner. Above all, where Frost tries to fit the cadences of common speech into the pattern of blank verse, Agee uses a consciously poetic diction to whip up a more violent poetic emotion; and where Frost, as Auden has pointed out, uses natural objects "not as foci for mystical meditation, but as things with which and on which man acts in the course of his daily gaining of a livelihood," [48] Agee uses them as natural symbols in order to reduce to poetically meaningful terms the nature of human existence. Still, the comparison with Frost is not without significance. Writing in a rural tradition, Frost was for long considered an unsophisticated poet, out of touch with the contemporary trends in modern poetry so closely allied to new research in anthropology, psychology, philosophy, or history. The same can be said about Agee. His peculiar talent for reducing the human situation not to its fashionable components in terms of modern science, but to its most elemental content, in terms of nature (albeit symbolically used), rather than in terms of political movements such as Communism or Socialism, and in terms of God, rather than in terms of anthropology (as Eliot seemed to have done in *The Waste Land*), made him strangely unfashionable in the eyes of his contemporaries. Above all, he had, as John M. Bradbury calls it, a "burning honesty and compulsive drive" [49] with strong overtones of moral effort simply as a *human* imperative rather than directed by the doctrines of popular movements.

It is impossible to know if Agee would ever have become a major poet had he concentrated more of his talents on verse. As this chapter has shown, he was acutely aware of the medium he was working in, he felt dissatisfied with traditional form and expressed a desire to write "musically" and to evolve a new kind of poetic diction. In this, he hardly succeeded, not because he lacked the talent, but because his ambition was so out of the ordinary and, also, because, as it turned out, prose proved to be a better medium for it than poetry. The early poetry simply shows a talented young man working with language, developing his skill in handling words, rhythms, images, and metaphors, and, above all, emotions. And all that is best in the poetry, the clear and precise language, the high rhetoric, the human involvement, the moral effort, the search for a huge symphonic structure accommodating the details of human experience, simple and complex, all looks forward to what he was to attempt more decisively in *Let Us Now Praise Famous Men*. The poetry, try as it may, does not entirely succeed in fusing that improbable combination of an Anglo-Catholic tradition and a Whitmaniacal "feeling of love for everything." As John Bradbury has pointed out, it "often sinks to the Stuart level in his effusive treatment of religious and sentimental themes," [50] but in "Dedication," where the Anglo-Catholicism is used as a perspective or a point of view rather than as a theme, Agee does succeed in building a "musical" structure with a powerful, reiterative impact in the manner of Whitman.

The Whitman influence, the idea of individual experience with close attention paid to all its details, is perhaps the most significant trait in the early poems. Not surprisingly, the title poem in *Permit Me Voyage* derives from another American poet who was also a visionary and who tried to create an American epic out of the diversity of American experience. The last line in that poem is taken directly from "Voyage III" by Hart Crane: "Permit me voyage, Love, into your hands." It is a poem of submission to "My sovereign God my princely soul / Whereon my flesh is priestly stole" (59); and the poet sets out on his symbolistic journey in full knowledge of the difficulty of the poet's task, of the untimeliness of his allegiance, of the debased state of the world, and with humility and faith toward his divine vision:

> [I know how] from the porches of our sky
> The crested glory is declined:
> And hear with what translated cry
> The stridden soul is overshined:
>
> And how this world of wildness through
> True poets shall walk who herald you:

Of whom God grant me of your grace
To be, that shall preserve this race.

Permit me voyage, Love, into your hands. (59)

The poem ends thus, seemingly unfinished, with one un-
rhymed line as a gangplank toward the future. That Agee
stayed faithful to that vision and that he was given the
grace to be among those true poets who "preserve this
race" in defending "the stridden soul" is demonstrated in
his later work.

II

AN EFFORT IN
HUMAN ACTUALITY

LET US NOW PRAISE FAMOUS MEN

The story of *Let Us Now Praise Famous Men*, James Agee's collaboration with Walker Evans, is by now so famous that it hardly needs repeating. It grew out of an assignment for *Fortune*, as a result of which Agee and Evans spent two months in the South studying and living with three tenant families in order to present a comprehensive report on the "sharecropping" problem. To Agee, the kind of article that *Fortune* demanded became increasingly difficult to write, and he was to labor with the work for a number of years and run into problems with its publication until it was finally brought out by Houghton Mifflin in 1941. Agee refused to see the problem in the simple economic and social terms which would make a readable article, and he recognized it instead as a moral confrontation; but this made the writing more difficult and expanded his subject matter to such an extent that anyone with less ambition than Agee might well have considered the task hopeless and given up. Agee, too, considered it hopeless, but he didn't give up; instead, he set out to make it a glorious failure. In August 1938, nearly two years after the original experience, he writes to Father Flye:

My trouble is, such a subject cannot be seriously looked at without intensifying itself toward a center which is beyond what I, or anyone else, is capable of writing of: the whole problem and nature of existence. Trying to write it in terms of moral problems alone is more than I can possibly do. My main hope is to state the central subject and my ignorance from the start, and to manage to indicate that no one can afford to treat any human subject more glibly or to act on any less would-be central basis: well, there's no use trying to talk about it. If I could make it what it ought to be made I would not be human.[1]

Five months later he is still wrestling with the problem of the morality of writing the kind of book he is trying for; he writes to Father Flye:

I made a try lately of writing the book in such language that anyone who can read and is seriously interested can understand it. I felt it was a failure and would take years to learn how to do but became so excited in it I had (and have) a hard time resuming my first method; including a sense of guilt. The lives of these families belong first (if to anyone) to people like them and only secondarily to the "educated" such as myself. If I have done this piece of spiritual burglary no matter in what "reverence" and wish for "honesty," the least I can do is to return the property where it belongs, not limit its language to those who can least know what it means. But I can't and should not sacrifice "educated" ideas and interests which the "uneducated" have no chance or reason, yet, to be other than bored by; and until I can keep these yet put them in credible language I guess there's nothing better I can do about it than write as to the "educated." Also in spite of intense convictions

I mistrust myself; and if you're going to write what may be poison better write it to adults than to perfectly defenseless children.[2]

When the book finally appeared, in 1941, the "share-cropping" problem no longer had the same urgency it had had in the thirties, and the critics, with a few notable exceptions, were confused, angry, or bored. *Time*'s reviewer found it "the most distinguished failure of the season," and while he recognized that "Agee's bad manners, exhibitionism and verbosity are a sort of author's curse at his own foredoomed failure to convey all he feels," and that the book contained "some of the most exciting U.S. prose since Melville," he was bored by "tedious stretches of self-indulged introspective and childish philosophy" and complained that Agee "clumsily intrudes between his subject and his audience even when the subject is himself." [3]

George Barker, in *The Nation*, found the book an "appalling inventory of the irrelevant, the incidental, and the relevant" and complained of its "pretentious whimsicality (a characteristic of a certain category of American literature for which the shade of Whitman ought to be impeached by the Society of American Authors)." [4] Harvey Breit, in *New Republic*, found the book rich and "many-eyed," and recognized that Agee's techniques suggest "the difficulties and the almost insurmountable ethical concerns the writer experienced in his relations with these men and women and children," but in spite of the good writing he felt that "there are too many tongues, too many attitudes, too many awarenesses on the subjective side (perhaps defenses would be more precise); even the sincerity is too much, too prostrate." [5]

The reviewer in *Commonweal* found the book "too

repetitious, too obscene, too obsessed with irrelevant details," and remarked on the "complete absence of discipline and form, whether literary, emotional, or intellectual";[6] this charge was echoed by the writer of a short note in *Library Journal*, who found the book "a mass of unrelated, nonsensical material, some parts almost the ravings of a lunatic, while others are beautiful, lyric prose of high merit, not entirely related to sharecropping. There are many objectionable passages and references."[7] Ruth Lechlitner, in the *New York Herald Tribune Books*, demanding that the author "must, because of the specific nature of his subject, communicate also in objective terms . . ." found Agee "not only a poet but a corking good journalist" although she thought it was a "mistake to try to combine . . . two separate approaches to a subject in one book."[8]

Paul Goodman, on the other hand, writing in *Partisan Review*, thought that "perhaps the best portions of the work are those very ones in which he describes his misgivings at being a spy and a stranger, his refusal to submit to the categories of sociology or the devices of drama, and (to my mind a place of intense beauty) the description of his guilty joy as he fine-combs the house when the family is away." Still, Goodman accused Agee of "reading into their situation his own qualities, frailties, and often prejudices," and found that "his passages on the poetics of what he is doing are confusion."[9] Apart from Lionel Trilling, who called the book "perhaps the most important moral effort of our American generation,"[10] one of the rare appreciative reviews came from Selden Rodman, who pointed out that "part of the greatness and unique quality of *Let Us Now Praise Famous Men*, then, is its structural failure, its overall failure as the 'work of art' it does not aim or presume to be and which from moment to moment it is . . . *Let*

Us Now Praise Famous Men will be spat upon—and years hence (unless the country is given over to the fascists or the faith-healers of 'far-away' democracy) read." [11]

These reviews show clearly that Agee was as untimely as ever: the thirties were over, and no matter how great the interest in sharecropping had been, it was not enough to condone, in 1941, Agee's original approach. Besides, Agee's book had an uncomfortable tendency to criticize both sides of the problem, both the socially progressive New Deal studies and the reactionary politics of landowners and Southerners. No wonder, then, that the book was a financial failure: as Dwight Macdonald has pointed out, "it sold less than six hundred copies the first year. *Moby Dick* sold five hundred, which was six times as good a showing, taking into account the increase of population." [12] The rest of the printing was slowly remaindered, but a small public kept discussing and praising the book, until, finally, Houghton Mifflin brought out a new printing in 1960. Although the reviews were still mixed, they were now more apt to call it a masterpiece of sorts, admitting that it was somewhat difficult to define exactly what sort it was. Mostly, reviewers chose to praise the splendid prose of the book, as, for instance, the *Time* reviewer did in noting that Agee had the artist's supreme gift, the ability to "bring even a reluctant reader into the heart of his own experience." [13]

Granville Hicks called the book "one of the extraordinary, one of the great books of our time," and suggested that the cumulative effects of Agee's lists of objects and words, in the end, is to "immerse us in the lives he is concerned with, and this, of course, is because he himself was so completely immersed." [14] Hicks, like many others, compared Agee to Melville, and Winfield Townley Scott made the same comparison, pointing out that the book "should have been cut, like *Leaves of Grass* and *Moby Dick*." Scott called the book a typical "American literary freak. And those, after all, are our greatest books." [15]

There was, however, still political dissent in some quarters: Priscilla Robertson, writing in *The Progressive*, pointed out that according to her experience, things had not really been as Agee saw them, and the situation had improved since the writing of the book simply because Americans helped themselves to overcome poverty and ignorance and disease. She was forced to conclude, therefore, that "James Agee couldn't imagine anyone's being either happy or self-propelled. He was a tragic poet who had to see and magnify and beautify into art the suffering in any life." [16] In a discussion of the resurgence of the twenties in the fifties and of the thirties in the sixties, E. Larsen seemed to come to a similar conclusion when he pointed out that " 'compassion' was a word read by him in its basic sense; he wanted to and needed to suffer with these people." [17]

Thus, most reviewers found the book extremely uneven although they recognized in it passages of great intensity as well as beauty and a strong (although highly personal and idiosyncratic) concern with a basic morality; but nobody really tried to see the work as a unity, structured in its peculiar way for a definite purpose instead of being merely a collection of fragmentary notes and reflections. One exception was Erik Wensberg, who, in *The Nation*, pointed to the very basic religious structure of the book as well as to the stylistic relationship with the Bible; he also found that "Agee's versatile prose is by turns minutely reportorial, 'magical' (in the painter's sense of that word) and lyric, stately as legend, and always, I think, to be regarded as being at a greater or lesser distance from the bardic, which is its natural mode." [18]

Let Us Now Praise Famous Men is, of course, an uncomfortably original work, and it is easier to say what it is not than what it is. It is not a novel, or a documentary, or a journal, or a philosophical treatise, or a sociological study. A work which so refuses to fall into any of the comfortable classifications must, by necessity, disturb the equilibrium of most critics. Nevertheless, it is surprising that so far nobody has attempted to define exactly what *Let Us Now Praise Famous Men* is through correlating Agee's explicit statements about the book (in the book) with the book as a whole. These statements begin in the preface and occur at spaced intervals all through the book; thus, they provide a clue to the intention of the author, which may be of assistance for the proper interpretation.

In the preface, after describing some of the history of the book and defining the nominal subject as North American cotton tenantry, Agee states clearly the basic intention of the work:

Actually, the effort is to recognize the stature of a portion of unimagined existence, and to contrive techniques proper to its recording, communication, analysis, and defense. More essentially, this is an independent inquiry into certain normal predicaments of human divinity. [19]

These two sentences accurately predict all of the preoccupations of Agee later in the book. The first sentence states the two basic concerns, and it is important to note the dual ambition since it explains so much of the structure of the work. Thus, although the effort "to recognize the stature of a portion of unimagined existence" sounds like a more than usually ambitious attempt to provide a documentary account of "sharecropping," the second concern, "to contrive techniques proper to its recording, communication, analysis, and defense," is equally important, as Agee puts it. And just as Agee prefers not to write a traditionally descriptive documentary study but recognizes the essentially moral duty in his investigation of *actual* lives ("recognize the stature"), so he realizes that this investigation must begin with the morality of the method of investigating and communicating itself. Thus the book not only deals with a specific subject but also discusses ways of dealing with that subject.

The second sentence, of course, simply states the expansion of the study "into certain normal predicaments of human divinity": thus, if the first aspect of the study is perceived as a deeply felt moral concern, that subject becomes finally a religious matter and the investigation itself an effort to recognize the sacredness and holiness of any and all individual human lives. This is hardly the kind of ambition one might expect in a study of what is commonly called an economic, sociological problem; and Agee even asks his reader to keep this divergence in the book in mind:

Since [the book] is intended, among other things, as a swindle, an insult, and a corrective, the reader will be wise to bear the nominal subject, and his expectation of its proper treatment, steadily in mind. For that is the subject with which the authors are dealing, throughout. If complications arise, that is because they are trying to deal with it not as journalists, sociologists, politicians, entertainers, humanitarians, priests, or artists, but seriously. (xv)*

In view of the frequency of this disclaimer throughout the

* Page references in parentheses refer, in this chapter, to *Let Us Now Praise Famous Men* (Boston: Houghton Mifflin Company 1960)

book, it is absurd that practically all reviews have criticized (or praised) the work on journalistic, sociological, political, or artistic grounds. Admittedly, such points of view are more convenient than an effort to find out what is meant by dealing with a subject "seriously." On the other hand, the seriousness of Agee's and Evans's attempt is part of what the book tries to discuss; and a book with this kind of dual ambition needs (not to say deserves) the cooperation of the reader:

This is a *book* only by necessity. More seriously, it is an effort in human actuality, in which the reader is no less centrally involved than the authors and those of whom they tell. (xvi)

Books are written by journalists, sociologists, or artists; but *Let Us Now Praise Famous Men* is first of all an "effort in human actuality," an attempt to approach and understand the lives of actual beings, and to communicate that understanding in moral terms. As such, it is finally a human gesture celebrating "the true weight of responsibility which each human being must learn to undertake for all others"; and the qualities of this work can be judged, not as those of a work of art or of a treatise of whatever science, but only as those of an action or a gesture.

The most common criticism leveled against *Let Us Now Praise Famous Men* is its apparent lack of organization or its "complete absence of discipline and form, whether literary, emotional or intellectual." [20] Even as sympathetic a critic as Dwight Macdonald calls it a "miscellaneous book" and "that extraordinary grab bag." [21] Erik Wensberg points out that it is structured as a religious service, with verses, preamble, inductions and recessional,[22] but although terms from the Mass, such as Introit and Gradual, are repeatedly used, the work as a whole does not follow any established church service structure.

However, the work is carefully structured and the final effect depends on the design of the whole. There are three major parts to the book: "Part One: A Country Letter"; "Part Two: Some Findings and Comments"; "Part Three: Inductions." Surrounding these parts is the framework called "On the Porch," the first and third parts of which appear as beginning and end to the work proper; the middle part of "On the Porch" splits "Part Two: Some Findings and Comments" in two: that is where the heart of the work as a whole is conceived to be. In fact, Agee states that "On the Porch" was written "to stand as the beginning of a much longer book, in which the whole subject would be disposed of in one volume. It is here intended still in part as a preface or opening, but also as a frame and as an undertone and as the set stage and center of action, in relation to which all other parts of this volume are intended as flashbacks, foretastes, illuminations and contradictions" (245). The three central parts are interrupted by two intermissions, the first one "Colon: Curtain Speech," the second "Intermission: Conversation in the Lobby." Immediately preceding Part One occur some short images which help define the themes and attitudes of the work; similarly, such images and notes occur immediately succeeding Part Three.

The structure of the book is largely symmetrical, describing in the main a movement reminiscent, say, of a Shakespearean five-act drama (as *Julius Caesar*), or a Beethoven symphony (the Fifth). The musical analogy is in fact relevant, for Agee also thought of his treatment as simple themes on four levels which would provide the kind of counterpoint and harmony found in music:

Very roughly I know that to get my own sort of truth out of
the experience I must handle it from four planes:

1   That of recall, of reception, contemplation, *in medias res*:
for which I have set up this silence under darkness on this
front porch as a sort of fore-stage to which from time to time
the action may have occasion to return.

2   'As it happened': the straight narrative at the prow as from
the first to last day it cut unknown water.

3   By recall and memory from the present: which is a part of
the experience: and this includes imagination, which in the
other planes I swear myself against.

4   As I try to write it problems of recording; which, too,
are an organic part of the experience as a whole.

These are, obviously, in strong conflict. So is any piece of
human experience. So, then, inevitably is any even partially
accurate attempt to give any experience as a whole. (243)

The novelist or, for that matter, the historian, generally
tries to make the past become the present, to make us see
it as happening; Agee, on the other hand, wants to use his
four planes to give the "experience as a whole," in its own
pastness:

It seems likely at this stage that the truest way to treat a piece
of the past is as such: as if it were no longer the present. In
other words, the 'truest' thing about the experience is now
neither that it was from hour to hour thus and so; nor is it my
fairly accurate 'memory' of how it was from hour to hour in
chronological progression; but is rather as it turns up in recall,
in no such order, casting its lights and associations forward
and backward upon the then past and the then future, across
that expanse of experience.

If this is so the book as a whole will have a form and set of
tones rather less like those of narrative than like those of music.
(243–44)

In other words, the truth of the experience cannot be expressed simply through a straight narrative but through a narrative which above all accepts the past as past, instead of giving it the value of a present which has somehow later disappeared. More seriously, this point of view implies a challenging of traditional forms of causality as it controls common types of narrative: since the act of recall changes the nature of the past experience itself, the writing becomes part of the experience and must be included in a narrative which tries to render the total truth. Thus, the emphasis on Agee's fourth level ("as I try to write it: problems of recording; which, too, are an organic part of the experience as a whole") is not motivated simply by a desire to discover the most moral means of communicating actuality but by a concept of the nature of experience itself.

Agee's suggestion that his treatment of themes occurs on four levels need not be taken at face value, but it should be taken seriously so far as it contributes something to the understanding of the work itself. Furthermore, in a work of this kind, the "intentional fallacy" [23] in its narrowest interpretation, does not make the analysis invalid: since the act of writing is an organic part of the experience the writer is trying to communicate in writing, his intention, insofar as he expresses it in his writing, is equally important. In other words, the explicitly stated intentions of the writer, as found in the book, are just as important as the results of those intentions whether the result is successful or not (and Agee repeatedly emphasizes that his task is a hopeless one and doomed to fail).

Trying, then, with the aid of this preliminary discussion to map out the structure of *Let Us Now Praise Famous Men*, we arrive at the following basic five-part construction:

OVERTURE

Mottos
Persons and Places
Verses
Preamble

Most important here is the "Preamble," which discusses the contrast "art—life" and establishes the problems and attitudes of the following investigation: Agee's Plane IV.

I

ON THE PORCH: 1

Three images: Late Sunday Morning
At the Forks
Near a Church

ON THE PORCH: 1 resumed (All over Alabama)

This section contains two lyrical pieces defining and approaching the sleeping earth; written on Plane I ("contemplation"), they surround three short straight narrative observations (Plane II: "as it happened") which have the common theme of definition of the narrator and his difficulties in communicating cleanly and clearly with the difficult situations confronting him. An attempt to approach.

II

PART ONE: A COUNTRY LETTER (Four movements)

In the first movement of this section, the narrator defines a human being and sees in relation to the night scene the family as a unit of cosmic loneliness, inevitably trapped by circumstances; this discussion, on Plane I, is complemented by the straight narrative of how one human being, the girl Emma, is trapped (Plane II).

The second movement, on Plane III, presents all the individuals in the area, their dreams and hopes and frustrations, in a counterpoint of short passages: the theme of loneliness and the individual trapped by circumstances is continued.

The third movement (Plane I) is an extremely dense dawn scene, describing nature's awakening and the agonizing ritual of getting up in the morning for the tenants (compared to serving at Mass early mornings): the theme of being trapped is echoed and continued.

The final movement is straight description, objective in tone and thus perhaps more of Plane II than of I, presenting how the men gather for work, trapped for another day.

The whole section, thus, leads up to the tenant's working day, having presented the individuals in an almost cosmic perspective, which defines their problem essentially as that of human existence.

COLON: CURTAIN SPEECH

This interruption is designed to show, first of all, the holiness and beauty of the individual soul as well as its circumscription and constant abuse by "life," and secondly, to discuss a means of trying to communicate as accurately as possible this situation. The narrative moves from Plane III to Plane IV: the narrator is constantly present.

III

A) PART TWO: SOME FINDINGS AND COM-
MENTS

   1) Money
   2) Shelter

B) *ON THE PORCH*: 2

C) PART TWO: SOME FINDINGS AND COM-
MENTS (cont'd)

   3) Clothing
   4) Education
   5) Work

This section is the heart of the work. It describes, on Plane III, the working day and conditions of the tenant farmer. *On the Porch: 2* discusses, on Plane IV, the most crucial aesthetic problems of how to write about and communicate the actuality of the lives of these tenant farmers.

INTERMISSION: CONVERSATION IN THE LOBBY

This interruption, a parallel to the Colon between II and III, consists of Agee's answers to a round question from *Partisan Review* in 1939 regarding the present state of American writing: on Plane IV, he deals mostly with the function of the artist in relation to truth and the past.

IV

PART THREE: INTRODUCTIONS

This section parallels II ("A Country Letter") in that its theme is that of approach: it begins with Psalm

43: "I will go unto the altar of God." Often couched in the form of a love letter to the family, it uses the terms of the Mass to show Agee in interaction with the tenants; the writing is mostly on Planes III and II.

V

Shady Grove, Alabama
Two images
Title Statement
Notes and Appendices
ON THE PORCH: 3

Like I, but in reverse order, this section uses sharp concrete images to sum up and define the concerns of the book ("Shady Grove": the inevitable end: death; "Two images": the broken yet vital humanity of two children; "Title Statement": an assertion from the Bible about the immortality of these people; "Notes and Appendices": a discussion of terms as well as the constant misuse of these terms, a fact which underlies the inability to solve, politically, the problem of the tenant farmers). *On the Porch: 3*, on Plane I, is a final, lyrical contemplation in which Agee finds "the frightening joy of hearing the world talk to itself, and the grief of incommunicability," yet realizes that the "ultimately hopeless effort" to communicate exactly and precisely all the joy, love and compassion of a human life "is not only beyond possibility but irrelevant to it."

This, then, is the structure on which the book is built. Yet, if this structure is simple to define in terms of rhetoric or simple classification and organization, any further discussion of the work (especially in literary terms) is complicated by at least two considerations.

The first is that according to the standards of the book, according to the most basic essence of what it is trying to communicate, any investigation such as the present one, dry-boned, analytic, intellectual, is by definition an insult to the book itself (which continually insists that it is *not* a work of art and a *book* only by necessity). A proper response to the book, again in its own terms, might be: to pray, to join the Peace Corps, to make love, to listen to Beethoven, to eat a good meal, to go without a meal, to paint a painting, or build a cathedral.

The second, which is related to the first, is that since the book does not claim to be a piece of literature, there are no characters to be discussed or analyzed; there are no or few actions to be given symbolic meaning. Everything that has substance in the book is actual, and that is its prime value. The characters, after all, cannot be criticized for being, independently of the book, alive and actual. Harvey Breit has tried to criticize the book on this basis; he writes: "These people are real, Mr. Agee insists, these people are *alive*. And yet it is the work itself that should make them so and not an *a-priori* statement." [24] Yet, while this criticism is perfectly valid in the case of, say, a novel, or any other fictional work, the enormousness of Agee's task in *Let Us Now Praise Famous Men* is due to the fact that these people are, *a priori*, alive and real. The writer's task is not primarily to make these people come alive in the novelist's sense of the word, but to approach them in such a way that he does not abuse or betray their actual existence. Alfred Kazin has commented briefly on the relationship of this kind of writing compared with that of ordinary documentaries:

Agee's text has a special importance not merely because it is an unusually sensitive document and a work of great moral intensity, but particularly because it represents a revolt against the automatism of the documentary school. It was begun as a typical documentary assignment and ended by being an attack on the facile mechanics and passivity of most documentary assignments. Agee went so far in his revulsion, in fact, that his book even took on the deep personal suffering of Faulkner's novels.[25]

Thus, while most journalists would consider their assignment a problem of how to put the material they have gathered in the most effective terms (which, ultimately, would have to be literary), Agee refuses to regard the tenant farmers as materials for a study but insists that they are a human reality to which one must respond. The questions of what response to accord a human reality cannot be answered in literary terms; since such a response must be measured in action, either latent or overt, it can only be evaluated or criticized in terms that are relevant to it as action—philosophy, morals, history, psychology.

What is implied in this kind of aesthetic is the relationship between art and life that the work itself tries to set up and the kind of genre its assumptions force it into. This is a question that concerns Agee all through the work itself. He writes, for instance: "Above all else: in God's name don't think of it as Art" (15); and the reason for this is not simply, as he says, that "every fury on earth has been absorbed in time, as art, or as religion, or as authority in one form or another" (15) but that the kind of communication that he desires is not so well achieved "by any means of art as through" what he calls "open terms" (12):

In a novel, a house or person has his meaning, his existence, entirely through the writer. Here, a house or a person has only the most limited of his meaning through me: his true meaning is much huger. It is that he *exists*, in actual being, as you do and as I do, and as no character of the imagination can possibly exist. His great weight, mystery, and dignity are in this fact. As for me, I can tell you of him only what I saw, only so accurately as in my terms I know how: and this in turn has its chief stature not in any ability of mine but in the fact that I too exist, not as a work of fiction, but as a human being. (12)

The kind of communication that would be most ideally suited to the material would not be writing at all:

If I could do it, I'd do no writing at all here. It would be photographs; the rest would be fragments of cloth, bits of cotton, lumps of earth, records of speech, pieces of wood and iron, phials of odors, plates of food and of excrement. Booksellers would consider it quite a novelty; critics would murmur, yes, but is it art; and I could trust a majority of you to use it as you would a parlor game.

A piece of the body torn out by the roots might be more to the point. (13)

Even so, the kind of writing that he is forced to undertake will have truth of its own:

If I bore you, that is that. If I am clumsy, that may indicate partly the difficulty of my subject, and the seriousness with which I am trying to take what hold I can of it; more certainly, it will indicate my youth, my lack of mastery of my so-called art or craft, my lack perhaps of talent. Those matters, too, must reveal themselves as they may. However they turn out, they cannot be otherwise than true to their conditions, and I would not wish to conceal these conditions even if I could, for I am interested to speak as carefully and as near truly as I am able. . . . I am no better an "artist" than I am capable of being, under these circumstances, perhaps under any other; and . . . this again will find its measurement in the facts as they are, and will contribute its own measure, whatever it may be, to the pattern of the effort and truth as a whole. (10–11)

Thus, in this kind of work in which the supreme effort to tell the absolute truth is made, the writer's failure to communicate it to his audience becomes itself an integral part of that truth. In one sense, paradoxically, failure seems to annihilate itself to become success, and in the same sense, Agee suggests, even "a falsehood is entirely true to those derangements which produced it and which made it impossible that it should emerge in truth; and an examination of it may reveal more of the 'true' 'truth' than any more direct attempt upon the 'true' 'truth' itself" (230).

The "true" "truth" is not simply that there exists, in the rural South, three specific tenant families with certain specific names and certain actual lives, but that there is a man called James Agee whose act of writing about these families we are constantly and immediately experiencing. This truth is in many ways different from the "truth" we find in works of art. On the one hand, this "truth" is just as valid a part of human experience as any other experience, and this is a strong argument "in favor of art which proves and asserts nothing but which exists, as has been dangerously guessed at, for its own sake." Agee draws the natural conclusion from this and asserts that "severe and otherwise insolvable human and spiritual problems are solved in every performance of, or for that matter in the silent existence of, say, Beethoven's quartet Opus 131" (231).

But while works of the imagination are to be valued and respected, because "in a certain degree they create something which has never existed before, they add to and somewhat clarify the sum total of the state of being, whereas the rest of the mind's activity is merely deductive, descriptive, acquisitive, or contemplative" and they thus "advance and assist the human race, and make an opening in the darkness around it, as nothing else can" (232), still "art and the imagination are capable of being harmful" (232). For one thing, the suspension of disbelief (which follows automatically with the reader's knowledge that the work of art is "made") "means that anything set forth within an art form, "true" as it may be in art terms, is hermetically sealed away from identification with everyday 'reality'" (240). And this is true even of the naturalist's art:

It is simply impossible for anyone, no matter how high he may place it, to do art the simple but total honor of accepting it and believing it in the terms in which he accepts and honors breathing, lovemaking, the look of a newspaper, the street he walks through. If you think of that a little while, and have any respect for art, and for what it is or should be capable of if it is to be held worthy of its own existence, that is a crucially serious matter. (240)

Furthermore, the artist who realizes the essential nature of language, namely that "words cannot embody: they can only describe," and tries to "bring words as near as he can to an illusion of embodiment," "accepts a false-

hood but makes, of a sort in any case, better art" (238).
This is an ambiguous achievement:

. . . art accepts the most dangerous and impossible of bargains
and makes the best of it, becoming, as a result, both nearer the
truth and farther from it than those things which, like science
and scientific art, merely describe, and those things which,
like human beings and their creations and the entire state of
nature, merely are, the truth.   (238)

The very selectivity which an artist accepts as necessary
for his craft makes even the "truest" and most "beautiful"
facts "lose so much of their force and reality" (241).

Agee argues consistently for a viewpoint which, in one
sense, equates art and life in assuming that the value of art
lies in its contribution to the area of human experience,
or life, and, in another sense, consistently chooses life, or
actuality, over the made-up reality of art: "I am in this
piece of work illimitably more interested in life than in
art" (242). This leads him into a position where he must
affirm not only that life can be more beautiful than art,
but also that it is identical with art:

How many, not only of the salient and obvious but more particularly of the casual passages in our experience, carry a value,
joy, strength, validity, beauty, wholeness, radiance, of which
we must admit not only that they equal in their worthiness as
a part of human experience, and of existence, the greatest
works of art but, quite as seriously, that the best art quite as
powerfully as the worst manages, in the very process of di-
gesting them into art, to distort, falsify and even to obliterate
them.   (232)

Similarly, he points out that everything in nature, "every
most casual thing, has an inevitability and perfection which

art as such can only approach, and shares in fact, not as art, but as the part of Nature that it is; so that, for instance, a contour map is at least as considerable an image of absolute 'beauty' as the counterpoints of Bach which it happens to resemble" (233). Since Agee makes no essential distinction between life and art, he sees no distinction between what he calls "intended" beauty and beauty achieved by chance. Or:

The Beethoven piano concerto #4 *IS* importantly, among other things, a "blind" work of "nature," of the world and of the human race; and the partition wall of the Gudgers' front bedroom *IS* importantly, among other things, a great tragic poem. (204)

One of the problems created by the kind of aesthetic that Agee seems to embrace is based on the fact that "words cannot embody; they can only describe" (238). This, of course, is also the reason for Agee's passionate approval of the art of photography: the photograph embodies reality in a sense in which words do not, and "handled cleanly and literally in its own terms" the camera is "incapable of recording anything but absolute, dry truth" (234). Words, on the other hand, are "the most inevitably inaccurate of all mediums of record and communication," troubled by "falsification (through inaccuracy of meaning as well as inaccuracy of emotion); and inability to communicate simultaneity with any immediacy" (236–37). The problem for the naturalist is that his extensive descriptions gather "time and weightiness" and sag "with this length and weight" (235). The only way to avoid this is to face radically the hopelessness of the task and the absolute inevitability of failure. "If, anti-artistically, you desire not only to present but to talk about what you present and how you try to present it, then one of your first anxieties, in advance of failure foreseen, is to make clear that a sin is a sin" (238). This sinfulness (or betrayal of the reality to be communicated) appears in the mere desire to talk about certain things as beautiful when they are necessities to the people who own them. But Agee insists:

> The beauty of a house inextricably shaped as it is in an economic and human abomination, is at least as important a part of the fact as the abomination itself: but . . . one faces the brunt of his own "sin" in so doing and the brunt of the meaning, against human beings, of the abomination itself. (203)

And, in a footnote, he adds: "The 'sin,' in my present opinion, is in feeling in the least apologetic for perceiving the beauty of the houses" (203).

In other words, the writer must accept himself as an inevitable presence in the book and assume a radical subjectivity in trying to describe events, persons, and things:

> George Gudger is a man, et cetera. But obviously, in the effort to tell of him (by example) as truthfully as I can, I am limited. I know him only so far as I know him, and only in those terms in which I know him; and all of that depends as fully on who I am as on who he is.
>
> I am confident of being able to get at a certain form of the truth about him, *only if* I am as faithful as possible to Gudger as I know him, to Gudger as, in his actual flesh and life (but there again always in my mind's and memory's eye) he is. But of course it will be only a relative truth.
>
> Name me one truth within human range that is not relative and I will feel a shade more apologetic of that. (239)

A few pages later, Agee adds:

I will be trying here to write of nothing whatever which did not in physical actuality or in the mind happen or appear; and my most serious effort will be, not to use these "materials" for art, far less for journalism, but *to give them as they are and as in my memory and regard they are.* (242)

This insistence on the inevitability and absoluteness on the subjective viewpoint leads him again to insist that *Let Us Now Praise Famous Men* is not a book:

It is simply an effort to use words in such a way that they will tell as much as I want to and can make them tell of a thing which happened and which, of course, you have no other way of knowing. It is in some degree worth your knowing what you can of not because you have any interest in me but simply as the small part it is of human experience in general. (246)

Thus, instead of a book, or a work of art, he has provided a small part of human experience. In this breakdown of all distinctions between art and life, Agee's book comes close to the kind of painting which in recent years has been called action painting, and a brief discussion of this phase of modern art will be helpful in trying to criticize Agee's work.

The innovation of action painting, as the critic Harold Rosenberg has pointed out in his excellent study *The Tradition of the New*, "was to dispense with the *representation* of the state [of the artist's psyche] in favor of *enacting* it in physical movement. The action on the canvas became its own representation." [26] Since action cannot be criticized in aesthetic terms, "what gives the canvas its meaning is not psychological data but *role*, the way the artist organizes his emotional and intellectual energy as if he were in a living situation." [27] The interest in the painting is thus primarily dramatic.

This kind of art demands a criticism able to recognize the assumptions underlying the "mode of creation" of the work. "Since the painter has become an actor, the spectator has to think in a vocabulary of action: its inception, duration, direction–psychic state, concentration and relaxation of the will, passivity, alert waiting. He must become a connoisseur of the gradations between the automatic, the spontaneous, the evoked." [28] It may seem difficult to formulate critical evaluations on this basis, but Rosenberg points out that seen in this perspective, "the test of any of the new paintings is its seriousness—and the test of its seriousness is the degree to which the act on the canvas is an extension of the artist's total effort to make over his experience." [29] And since the painting is conceived in terms of action and decision, there is even a moral element to be considered:

action painting has extracted the element of decision inherent in all art in that the work is not finished at its beginning but has to be carried forward by an accumulation of "right" gestures. In a word, action painting is the abstraction of the *moral* element in art; its mark is moral tension in detachment from moral or esthetic certainties; and it judges itself morally in declaring that picture to be worthless which is not the incorporation of a genuine struggle, one which could at any point have been lost.[30]

Although there are, obviously, a good many distinctions to be made between *Let Us Now Praise Famous Men* and an action painting, the critical method outlined by Rosenberg is the only possible meaningful way of regarding Agee's work. The theme of the work as a whole is the writer's effort to approach reality (or, for that matter, actuality); and this theme exists on two levels: first, that of approaching real, alive, actual, specific human beings and things, such as the Gudger family and their house; second, that of approaching the reality of words and language. In fact, the encounter of the writer with reality is entirely and exactly comparable to his encounter with language. In both cases, there exists a problem of communication, of understanding and of being understood; on both levels, there is a constant struggle to master the responsibilities of the material of the situation, i.e., first to comprehend the actuality and reality of these actual farmers as accurately and completely as possible, and second, to write as truly as possible about the experiences. To suggest that one of these struggles is moral (or political) and the other artistic is meaningless. It is possible to suggest that (1) the writer's encounter with "reality" results in a human action (of one kind or another, maybe even psychological), and that (2) the writer's encounter with language results in a book. But in these two sentences, the words "human action" and "book" are interchangeable. The book is just as much a result of the writer's encounter with "reality" as the "human action" is a result of his encounter with words, and vice versa. Thus, the struggle to write the book is no less a moral or political effort than the encounter in the rural South. In both cases, too, the result is actual and immediate and irrevocable: the encounter with the farmers has immediate results in experience, and the writing of the book results in the same kind of immediacy of experience (since even a failure would not change the essential nature of the task and thus would still be a part of the original experience). And both encounters are, to use Rosenberg's words, struggles "which could at any point have been lost." [31] In fact, the struggle is won not only by a recognition of the inevitability of failure or by resisting the temptation of failure ("Failure, indeed, is almost as strongly an obligation as an inevitability, in such work; and therein sits the deadliest trap of the exhausted conscience" [32]) but by realizing that failure is irrelevant to the essence of the experience itself, and that the "ultimately hopeless effort" would be "above most efforts, so useless" (470).

This, then, is the aesthetic of the "effort in human actuality," and one reason for examining it so carefully is that ordinary literary terms, such as structure, symbol, imagery, style, acquire new meanings in new contexts. Regarding *Let Us Now Praise Famous Men* as an action or a human gesture, what, exactly, is the structure of an action? What is its theme and its style? Such questions are tenuous, at best, but they can be given a reasonable amount of meaning if an action is defined, say, as the manifestation of a moment of choice or of the actor's organization of emotional, intellectual, and other energies. An action, as such, does not have a structure: as manifestation it may have a chronological progression, although its immediacy as action is simple rather than complex. But, as Rosenberg points out, what gives the action meaning is *"role,* the way the artist organizes his emotional and intellectual energy as if he were in a living situation." [33] The interest in this *role,* thus, becomes primarily dramatic, observing the development of the author, not as character, not as person, but as actor on the arena of language and words. It is worth noting here that Agee himself, asserting the validity of landscape painting as a human activity, points out that

"Cocteau, writing of Picasso and of painting, remarks that the subject is merely the excuse for the painting, and that Picasso does away with the excuse" (239). And Rosenberg has pointed out that Picasso's objection to formalist criticism, opening the way for art as action, substitutes the dramatics of the role; he quotes Picasso as saying: "What forces our interest is Cézanne's anxiety—that's Cézanne's lesson; the torments of Van Gogh—that is the actual drama of the man. The rest is sham." [34]

If, then, the action is given meaning by the role which it helps define, it can also be said that the role is defined by everything that leads up to and contributes to it—and this includes psychology, morality, sociology, religion, biology, even chance. And these things are seen not only in the explicit comments of the writer, but also in such literary traits as imagery, style, levels of narrative, and so on. Thus, while the structure of the action is impossible to get at with ordinary critical tools, a literary analysis is significant insofar as it helps define the role of the artist (or non-artist) in simply human terms.

The first, preliminary sections of the book, the preface and what I have called the overture (mottos, list of persons, and the preamble), are dominated by a mood of belligerence and sometimes deliberate insult. Besides stating simply the theme of the book, Agee points out that it is intended as a "swindle" and an "insult" (xv); and in the list of characters, as well as in the preamble, he calls himself and Evans spies or counterspies. In the list he also presents Blake, Celine, Lardner, Christ, Freud, Lonnie Johnson, Irving Upham, and others, presumably members of the cast of the story, as "unpaid agitators."

The work as a whole has two mottos: the first is King Lear's famous speech on the heath in the third act: "Poor naked wretches, wheresoe'er you are . . ."; the second is the words of the *Communist Manifesto:* "Workers of the world, unite and fight. You have nothing to lose but your chains, and a world to win." Obviously, the juxtaposition of the two quotations is designed to shock the complacent reader; and Agee goes even further when he asserts, in a footnote, that "these words are quoted here to mislead those who will be misled by them." One might well ask, as at least one critic, with some justification, has done: what on earth for? The point, of course, is that those who want to be misled will always find something to be misled by; those who like to label movements, those who choose the facile interpretations, those who profess their profound interest in and concern for certain questions without going beyond the superficial and the sophisticated, will always fail to realize that words such as those quoted may, as Agee states, "mean, not what the reader may care to think they mean, but what they say." In a sense, Agee is here, although on a different level, warning against the same mistake he warns against throughout the book, namely that of mistaking actual reality for an abstract fiction.

In the same footnote, Agee declares that the first quotation from *King Lear* and the second from the *Manifesto* are, in the pattern of the work as a whole, "in the sonata form," the first and the second theme respectively. The first theme, then, is the narrator's effort to experience, in realistic terms, the actuality of a certain portion of un-imagined existence: "Take physick, pomp; Expose thyself to feel what wretches feel, / That thou may'st shake the superflux to them, / And show the heavens more just." The second theme, quite simply, indicates the author's awareness of and concern for the workers of the world and his realization that their plight has to be alleviated in one way or another. But Agee's distrust of his readers and his awareness of the resistance to his effort lead him to add that "in view of the average reader's tendency to label, and of topical dangers to which any man, whether honest, or intelligent, or subtle, is at present liable, it may be well to make the explicit statement that neither these words nor the author's are the property of any political party, faith, or faction." Despite the correctness of the diction and the neutrality of style in this sentence, there is in these words a latent hostility toward the average reader as well as a realization of the almost automatic misunderstanding of almost any statement.

The tone which defines the role of the narrator in the introductory section is one of distrust toward the reader and the task confronting him; this distrust (and the consequent realization of the inevitability of failure) also tempers the fury of the writer's ambition, although, instead of tempting him into a compromise, it merely intensifies the fury and increases the demands he is willing to make on the reader (and so, incidentally, making failure even more inevitable). Thus, Agee advises the reader to listen to a record of Beethoven's Seventh Symphony or Schubert's C Major Symphony turned on as loud as possible, ears as close into the loudspeaker as they can get, because under such conditions, "as near as you will ever get, you are inside the music; not only inside it, you are it; your body is no longer your shape and substance, it is the shape and substance of the music" (16). This intensity of perception which Agee sets as a goal for himself (as well as for the reader) throughout the book (cf. pp. 38–39, 57–58, 183–84), and which is foreshadowed in a remarkable line in a letter to Father Flye in February 1936, "Things have to be believed with the body or in other

-words soul, not just perceived of the mind," [35] is dangerous and unsettling because it leads to a heightened awareness of a dimension of truth:

Is what you hear pretty? or beautiful? or legal? or acceptable in polite or any other society? Is it beyond any calculation savage and dangerous and murderous to all equilibrium in human life as human life is; and nothing can equal the rape it does on all that death; nothing except anything, anything in existence or dream, perceived anywhere remotely toward its true dimension. (16)

This fury also leads Agee to call Beethoven's statement, "He who understands my music can never know unhappiness again," a "rash and noble" saying, and to use the same words for his own perception and intention. The only goal worth aiming for is the highest one that ambition can envision, no matter how clear one's realization that "performance, in which the whole fate and terror rests, is another matter" (16).

The first proper section of the book contains two lyrical "contemplations" ("On the Porch: 1") surrounding three straight short narratives ("Sunday Morning," "At the Forks," "Near a Church"). Its theme is that of a slow approach and the difficulty of communication. The lyrical night-pieces are dominated by images of night, darkness, sleep, nature, earth, sky, planets, animals; the effect is that of moving the narrative back to the earliest beginning of creation:

On some ledge overleaning that gulf which is more profound than the remembrance of imagination they had lain in sleep and at length the sand, that by degrees had crumpled and rifted, had broken from beneath them and they sank. There was now no further extreme, and they were sunken not singularly but companionate among the whole enchanted swarm of the living, into a region prior to the youngest quaverings of creation. (21)

In keeping with this primeval setting as well as the personification of the sky as a woman (21), the concluding lyric night-picture of Birmingham personifies the whole American continent:

"Beneath, the gulf lies dreaming, and beneath, dreaming, that woman, that id, the lower American continent, lies spread before heaven in her wealth" (45). It is out of this primeval night that the people will eventually emerge: it is here that they are born just as in one of the final vignettes, "Shady Grove Alabama," they are laid to rest. Thus, in this early section, Agee's imagery suggests some of the dominant movements of the work as a whole: the chronology of a human life, from birth to death; the chronology from deepest night through dawn into full day and back to night.

The three narrative pieces share the theme of the impossibility of communicating the most important things. In the first piece, a white landowner orders a Negro quartet to sing for Agee and Evans:

. . . and during all this singing, I had been sick in the knowledge that they felt they were here at our demand, mine and Walker's, and that I could communicate nothing otherwise; and now, in a perversion of self-torture, I played my part through. I gave their leader fifty cents, trying at the same time, through my eyes, to communicate much more. (31)

In the second piece, Agee confronts some extremely poor farmers to ask directions; after a short conversation about their situation, he tells them good-bye: "I had not the heart at all to say, Better luck to you, but then if I remember rightly I did say it, and, saying it or not, and unable to communicate to them at all what my feelings were, I walked back the little distance to the car with my shoulders and the back of my neck more scalded-feeling than if the sun were on them" (37). In the third piece, Agee runs after a young Negro couple to ask information and realizes suddenly that the young woman is scared to death of whatever he might do, as a white person, and he tries to reassure them:

I thanked them very much, and was seized once more and beyond resistance with the wish to clarify and set right, so that again, with my eyes and smile wretched and out of key with all I was able to say, I said I was awfully sorry if I had bothered them; but they only retreated still more profoundly behind their faces, their eyes watching mine as if awaiting any sudden move they must ward, and the young man said again that that was all right, and I nodded, and turned away from them, and walked down the road without looking back. (43)

Besides stating the basic theme, these three pieces also help to define the narrator and some of his attitudes. There is, for instance, a first concrete example of the kind of physical perception of reality, which has been discussed in the preamble (39); there is also, in the description of the farming couple in "At the Forks," an example of Agee's ability to see not only a classical beauty (often exceeding that of "true" art) but also a sort of holiness in the simplest and poorest objects and surroundings: "There was in their eyes so quiet and ultimate a quality of hatred, and contempt, and anger, toward every creature in existence beyond themselves, and toward the damages they sustained, as shone scarcely short of a state of beatitude; nor did this at any time modify itself" (33). Similar to this is his recognition of the natural grace and dignity of what seems like a purely animal existence: "their extreme dignity, which was as effortless, unvalued, and undefended in them as the assumption of superiority which suffuses a rich and social adolescent boy" (40); and the "sinfulness" of observing such things adds a further complexity to the experience which is likewise recorded: "I could not bear that they should receive from me any added reflection of the shattering of their grace and dignity, and of the nakedness and depth and meaning of their fear, and of my horror and pity and self-hatred" (41–42).

This first proper section of the book differs, above all, in tone from the introductory pieces; whereas the introductory tone is one of belligerence and stubborn fury, here Agee approaches his material with a quiet humility which is not essentially marred by his realization that humility is not enough:

The least I could have done was to throw myself flat on my face and embrace and kiss their feet. That impulse took hold of me so powerfully, from my whole body, not by thought, that I caught myself from doing it exactly and as scarcely as you snatch yourself from jumping from a sheer height; here, with the realization that it would have frightened them still worse (to say nothing of me) and would have been still less explicable; so that I stood and looked into their eyes and loved them, and wished to God I was dead. (42)

Above all, a passage such as this one indicates Agee's willingness to listen to and receive with almost physical immediacy the essential nature of his perception, as well as his awareness that this perception must be coupled with close observance of the purely subjective aspects of the experience.

The second major section of the book ("Part One: A Country Letter") moves from night through dawn into full morning, and thus serves to bring the reader up to the full working day of the tenant farmers. For the most part, it consists of the kind of lyrical prose which is Agee's first plane ("contemplation, *in medias res*"); in one place, it is interrupted by a straight narrative looking into the future ("you mustn't be puzzled by this, I'm writing in a continuum"—62); one of the four movements is an imaginative juxtaposition of the dreams and frustrations of the families, and this approaches Agee's third plane ("recall and memory from the present," including imagination).

The theme of the section is metaphorically stated in the prelude to the four movements: after closely observing and describing the lamp which illuminates his dark room, Agee writes:

. . . in this globe like a thought, a dream, the future, slumbers the stout-weft strap of wick, and up this wick is drawn the oil, toward heat; through a tight, flat tube of tin, and through a little slotted smile of golden tin, and there ends fledged with flame, in the flue; the flame, a clean, fanged fan. (50)

The globe image is central to the section: it suggests not only the earth as planet: "we, this Arctic flower snow-rooted, last matchflame guarded on a windy plain, are seated among these stars alone: none to turn to, none to make us known; a little country settlement so deep, so lost in shelve and shade of dew, no one so much as laughs at us" (53); but also the family circle: "And thus, too, these families, not otherwise than with every family in the earth, how each, apart, how inconceivably lonely, sorrowful, and remote" (53); as well as the individual: "people are drawn inward within their little shells of rooms, and are to be seen in their wondrous and pitiful actions through the surfaces of their lighted windows by thousands, by millions, little golden aquariums . . . and none can care beyond that room; and none can be cared for, by any beyond that room" (54). In the interlude succeeding this section, Agee explains the image more explicitly in discussing how best to construct the kind of account the farmers deserve:

I might suggest, its structure should be globular: or should be eighteen or twenty intersected spheres, the interlockings of bubbles on the face of a stream; one of these globes is each of you.
    The heart, nerve, center of each of these, is an individual human life. (101)

There is a pattern of movement within the globes and among the globes: "the children are held to a magnetic center" (55), but later move away to form another globe:

. . . these flexions are taking place everywhere, like a simultaneous motion of all the waves of the water of the world: and these are the classic patterns, and this is the weaving, of human living: of whose fabric each individual is a part.   (56)

Here, two more important images are introduced that will recur throughout the book. The sea image stands for the vastness of the land which "is stretched like that hollow and quietness of water that is formed at the root of a making wave" (85), and when dawn comes over the land, "it is the indistinguishable and whispered sign of all the generations of the dead, the crumbling of a world-long wave so distant, that one yard more removed, could not be audible" (85). While the sea image is used to convey the vast stretch of human experience in its most elementary terms, the weaving image is used throughout the book to suggest the intricate pattern of interlocking relationships of various kinds: "A chain of truths did actually weave itself and run through: it is their texture that I want to represent, not betray, nor pretty up into art" (240).

Agee uses the image of the globe to suggest the infinite and inevitable loneliness of each individual, each family, or even each planet. And each of these has to sustain the "enormous assaults of the universe":

So that's how it can be that a stone, a plant, a star, can take on the burden of being; and how it is that a child can take on the burden of breathing; and how through so long a continuation and cumulation of the burden of each moment one on another, does any creature bear to exist, and not break utterly to fragments of nothing: these are matters too dreadful and fortitudes too gigantic to meditate long and not forever to worship. (56–57)

This is a more explicit statement of the theme of this section: each individual is inevitably trapped and abused by the "cumulation of the burden of each moment," and after his long meditation on these conditions of human existence, Agee proceeds to give a specific example: the story of the young girl, Emma, whose marriage at sixteen has trapped her into a life she can hardly bear. Whereas the first lyrical definition of human loneliness is written on the first plane, as contemplation and meditation, the story of Emma is told on the second plane, "as it happened," with much attention given to the relationship between Agee himself and Emma. Thus, the lyricism of an abstract meditation is immediately converted into the agony of a personal relationship, in which it is impossible to communicate all the emotion felt: "(that is always characteristic, I guess, of the seizure of the strongest love you can feel: pity, and the wish to die for a person, because there isn't anything you can do for them that is at all measurable to your love)" (64–65). The movement is then concluded with a long, tender description of the family getting ready for bed; and, finally, a two-page sentence punctuated only with colons and semicolons imitates the slow, tired action of getting into bed and slowly settling tired bodies to rest for the night.

The second movement of this section is written on Agee's third plane: it uses imaginative insights to present the dreams, hopes and frustrations of the people in a counterpoint of short passages and statements. The burden, or refrain, of the movement is the question: "In what way were we trapped? where, our mistake? what, where, how, when, what way, might all these things have been different, if only we had done otherwise? if only we might have known." (78) "How did we get caught?" (80) "How were we caught . . . How was it we were caught?" (81). Then, to conclude, Agee quotes the Beatitudes from the Sermon on the Mount. The whole movement is an imaginative extension, on another plane of narrative, of the theme presented in the first movement: where the first movement presented an abstract contemplative definition of human isolation and loneliness, with a specific example as an illustration, the second movement presents nearly all the characters of the book participating in an imaginative chorus on the main theme.

The third movement is a dawn scene which begins by observing continents awakening ("Spired Europe is out, up the middle of her morning . . . the Atlantic globe is burnished, ship-crawled . . . shoulder clean shoulder from their hanger, Brazil and Labrador"–83) and moves ("and so must these: while the glistening land drives east: they shall be drawn up like plants"–83) to the rural South ("The land, pale fields, black cloudy woodlands, and the late lamps in the central streets of the rare and inexpiable cities: New Orleans; Birmingham; whose façades stand naked in the metal light of their fear"–85) and on to the farmers themselves ("But much earlier, while it was not yet light, at about the crowing of the second cock, Annie Mae woke, on her back, and watched up at the ceiling"–87). The main theme of isolation, of being trapped, is emphasized in the description of the ritual of preparing breakfast according to the set pattern of every morning; at the same time, this ritual is compared to "earliest lonely Mass" (89): "it is in no beauty less than the gestures of a day here begin; and in just such silence and solitude" (89). At the end of the movement, "the houses are broken open like pods in the increase of the sun" (91); the farmers have been "drawn up like plants with the burden of being upon them" (83); and the plant imagery serves to emphasize the fact that this existence is dominated by nature and the seasons to such an extent that it is more of a trap than an environment.

The final movement is short and objective in tone; it describes the men gathering for work, harnessing the mules, and finally moving off. Here, the mules carry the main theme: the imagery presents them as "very naked-looking and somehow shy without harness, as if they had not quite the right to nature" (93); a white mule among them is likened to an "enslaved unicorn" (93), and when they are all harnessed, Agee calls them "the trapped mules" (94).

As a whole, then, this section, first of all, moves us from dark night through dawn into full morning and prepares us for the working day of the tenants. Secondly, it presents some of these actual lives as variations on the theme of individuals trapped and abused by the burden of being. Thirdly, the whole section is an attempt to comprehend these lives, physically as well as imaginatively, as emblems of human existence in general. The images of the sea, of plants and of nature (as well as, for that matter, the religious allusions) show these individuals as abused by existence in general rather than specifically by the situation in the rural South.

That specification is begun in the following section, "Colon," which Agee calls a "Curtain Speech." This section is an attempt to outline all the pressures on an individual that form him and try to suggest how they should be presented in a book of this kind. It begins with a definition of a soul, which uses religious imagery to suggest the sacredness of every individual:

. . . the human "soul," that which is angry, that which is wild, that which is untamable, that which is healthful and holy, that which is competent of all advantaging within hope of human dream, that which most marvelous and most precious to our knowledge and most extremely advanced upon futurity of all flowerings within the scope of creation is of all these the least destructible, the least corruptible, the most defenseless, the most easily and multitudinously wounded, frustrate, prisoned, and nailed into a cheating of itself: so situated in the universe that those three hours upon the cross are but a noble and too trivial an emblem how in each individual among most of the two billion now alive and in each successive instant of the existence of each existence not only human being but in him the tallest and most sanguine hope of godhead is in a billionate choiring and drone of pain of generations upon generations unceasingly crucified and is bringing forth crucifixions into their necessities and is each in the most casual of his life so measurelessly discredited, harmed, insulted, poisoned, cheated, as not all the wrath, compassion, intelligence, power of rectification in all the reach of the future shall in the least expiate or make one ounce more light.   (100)

It is in this mood of helpless fury and anger too that Agee conceives of the beginning of a soul as still another crucifixion:

Here we have two, each crucified, further crucify one another upon the shallow pleasure of an iron bed and instigate in a woman's belly a crucifixion of cell and whiplashed sperm: . . . in this instant already his globe is rounded upon him and is his prison, which might have been his kingdom.   (103-104)

Seeing, then, the individuals as "bubbles on the face of a stream" (101), Agee suggests how, from the beginning, this creature is abused, misused, tortured, deceived, paralyzed, and destroyed from all sides. Then, more specific tortures and abuses need to be defined as the individual is specialized:

. . . yes, he is of the depth of the working class; of southern alabamian tenant farmers; certain individuals are his parents, not like other individuals, they are living in a certain house, it is not quite like other houses . . . all such things as these qualify this midge, this center, a good deal.   (107)

The more the individual is specialized, the wider becomes the range of specific experiences and surroundings which have to be defined in order to present that individual adequately: "for of all these each is a life, a full universe" (110). The technical problem of thus presenting an individual in his full complexity is impossible to solve:

All this, all such, you can see, it so intensely surrounds and takes meaning from a certain center which we shall be unable to keep steadily before your eyes, that should be written, should be listed, calculated, analyzed, conjectured upon, as if all in one sentence and spread suspension and flight or fugue of music: and that I shall not be able so to sustain it, so to sustain its intensity toward this center human life, so to yield it out that it all strikes inward upon this center at once and in all its intersections and in the meanings of its inter-relations and inter-enchancements: it is this which so paralyzes me: yet one can write only one word at a time, and if these seem lists and inventories merely, things dead unto themselves, devoid of mutual magnetisms, and if they sink, lose impetus, meter, intension, then bear in mind at least my wish, and perceive in them and restore them what strength you can of yourself: for I must say to you, this is not a work of art or of entertainment, nor will I assume the obligations of the artist or entertainer, but this is a human effort which must require human co-operation. (111)

The purpose of this section is to prepare the reader for the infinitely specified account of the tenant farmer's working day in the following section. As such, it is, as Agee says, "all one colon" (110); just as in a sentence, it is the pause which introduces the more explicit examples: it is "a sharp end and clean silence: a steep and most serious withdrawal: a new and more succinct beginning" (99). In Agee's case, it is also the moment of hesitation in the realization of foredoomed failure: yet the attempt is made. Finally, more than any other mark of punctuation,

the colon suggests a kind of continuum, a logical relationship between what precedes and follows it; most other
marks separate rather than relate. Thus Agee's "Colon"
serves as a transition leading into the following section
at the same time that it presents the justification for the
kind of writing that is to follow.

The third section ("Part Two: Some Findings and
Comments") is, as has been stated earlier, the center of
the work. It tries to observe as closely and carefully as
possible the elements of the tenant farmer's working day.
In the middle, it is interrupted by the second installment
of *On the Porch*, which discusses the most difficult of the
technical and aesthetic problems confronting a writer of
this kind of book. The tone of the whole section is pre-
dominantly objective.

The division of the material is interesting, in that Agee
spends seven pages on "Money" (having, as he states it,
sacrificed a much longer chapter), a hundred pages on
"Shelter," and thirty pages each on "Clothing," "Education," and "Work." A more average study of sharecropping would presumably have devoted most of its interest
to money or work; to Agee the house is almost the most
revealing thing in the life of the tenants: "a human shelter,
a strangely lined nest, a creature of killed pine, stitched
together with nails into about as rude a garment against
the hostilities of heaven as a human family may wear"
(137); and when he concludes the description of the
houses, he sees that "upon the leisures of the earth the
whole home is lifted before the approach of darkness as a
boat and as a sacrament" (220). The investigation of the
house becomes, in effect, a metaphorical Mass, prefaced
"I will go unto the altar of God" (123), describing the
mantelpiece as the "altar" (162), and a table drawer as

"the tabernacle" (165), and ending with a recessional.

The hundred pages devoted to "Shelter" are, in fact, the most interesting part of the book because they seem to embody the work as a whole: they contain both accurate perception and reporting and discussions of the aesthetics and morality of the undertaking; in other words, they both try to "recognize the stature of a portion of unimagined existence, and to contrive techniques proper to its recording, communication, analysis, and defense" (xvi). Also, they employ most of the levels of narrative that are used in the book as a whole.

The purpose of the section is to approach as accurately as possible, physically and morally, the human actuality embodied by the house. The approach is begun from the fields, which are compared to "the spread and broken petals of a flower whose bisexual center is the house" (129). From that distance, the farm appears as "a water spider whose feet print but do not break the gliding water membrane" or as "the wrung breast of one human family's need and of an owner's taking, yielding blood and serum in its thin blue milk, and the house, the concentration of living and taking, is the cracked nipple" (129). This description of the fields leads into some short introductory comments about the beauty and "sorrowful holiness" (134) of the house and about how "this beauty is made between hurt but invincible nature and the plainest cruelties and needs of human existence in this uncured time, and is inextricable among these, and as impossible without them as a saint born in paradise" (134). Here, too, Agee recognizes that "the whole problem, if I were trying fully to embody the house, would be to tell of it exactly in its ordinary terms." (134). The description of the house itself is introduced with a short section presenting the memories of guilt and shame in the writer from his childhood, memories evoked by his now "being made witness to matters no human being may see" (136). Then follows an extremely detailed description of the house itself, commenting on the kind of wood used, its texture, look, smell, and general suitability as building material, listing the contents of table drawers to the last trivial detail. The description is interrupted for a brief consideration of the kind of physical perception which is impossible to communicate (but essential for a total embodying of what is perceived): first of all, it is possible "to realize for a little while at a time the simultaneity in existence of all of [the] rooms in their exact structures and mutual relationships in space and in all they contain; and to realize this not merely with the counting mind, nor with the imagination of the eye, which is no realization at all, but with the whole of the body and being . . ." (183); secondly, it is possible in a room where the materials are bare "to let all these things, each in its place, and all in their relationships and in their full substances, *be, at once*, driven upon your consciousness, one center: and there is here such an annihilating counterpoint as might be if you could within an instant hear and be every part, from end to end, of the most vastly spun of fugues . . ." (183). This is, of course, almost a mystic state, impossible to communicate in words, but, as has been pointed out in the discussion of the aesthetics of the book, the *description* of the intention becomes in this particular book just as important as the realization of that intent.

Then the family returns, and although his investigation has been "reverently" conducted, Agee feels guilt and shame for having, in a way, penetrated the private secrets of these actual lives. He concludes the section with brief discussions of the two other farm houses, some notes on beauty and the morality of observing beauty in the barest necessities of life and on isolated aspects of the kind of living these houses provide, and a "recessional and vortex" which lists the animals and plants and all the rest which "is sewn into these human lives" (218).

It should be clear from this summary that in its oscilla- tion between the recording of perceptions and the discus- sion of the morality and problems of preceiving and re- cording, this section epitomizes the character of the work as a whole. This is true also of the imagery, which is primarily derived from nature, animal life, the sea, religion, and music (in discussions of beauty or "beauty").

The essays on "Clothing," "Education," and "Work" are less intricately designed but just as difficult to discuss. It is easy, for example, to point out that the imagery, here too, derives from animals, nature, and, in the case of "beauty," from art: discussing overalls, Agee points to "the swift, simple, and inevitably supine gestures of dressing and of undressing, which, as is less true of any other gar- ment, are those of harnessing and of unharnessing the shoulders of a tired and hard-used animal" (266), and this, in the context of these lives, is a "meaningful" image; describing the texture of shirts, Agee can write:

. . . this fabric breaks like snow, and is stitched and patched: these break, and again are stitched and patched and ruptured, and stitches and patches are manifolded upon the stitches and patches, and more on these, so that at length, at the shoulders. the shirt contains virtually nothing of the original fabric and a man, George Gudger, I remember so well, and many hun- dreds of others like him, wears in his work on the power of his shoulders a fabric as intricate and fragile, and as deeply in honor of the reigning sun, as the feather mantle of a Toltec prince. (268)

This, too, is impressive, in a literary way, but its peculiar effect derives not from the slightly overelaborated prose considered as literature but from the fact that this is an effort to perceive as closely as possible an *actual* shirt. Agee's long descriptions of hats, overalls, shoes, dresses, as well as his intense descriptions of the physical effects of working in the cotton fields, are really too long, too overblown, and too minutely detailed to be functional as literature, but, as they stand, they present the actuality of the tenants' lives in the minutest and most insignificant (and thus unliterary) details. Above all, the significance and morality of this whole section resides in the effort to partake as intensely as possible, physically and imaginatively, of these actual lives; and, regarded this way, the *role* of the writer is seen, not as that of a snoopy maker of inventories, but as that of a man trying to recognize the totality of human experience in the specificity of one actual situation.

The next large section of the book, "Intermission," which consists of Agee's answers to a questionnaire from *Partisan Review* on "Some Questions Which Face American Writers Today," is a parallel to "Colon," first of all in its function as a withdrawal from the intensity of the previous section, and secondly, in its attempt to explain the predicament of the writer as *actor* in words. "Colon" is subtitled "Curtain Speech," and "Intermission" labeled "Conversation in the Lobby."

Most of the literary problems discussed have already, in one way or another, been made clear in previous sections. It is, however, significant, that Agee reacts with such anger to the question of a "usable" past and suggests that "all of the past one finds useful is 'usable' because it is of the present and because both present and past are essentially irrelevant to the whole manner of 'use' " (353). And just as he refuses to "use" material for literature, so he accepts a totality of experience in choosing models: " 'Usable': Every good artist; every record of the past; and more particularly, all of the present and past which exists in the 'actual,' 'unrecreated' world of personal or speculative experience" (353). And he goes on to list such good artists as Christ, Blake, Brady, everybody's letters, family albums, postcards, Melville, Joyce, Chaplin, Walker Evans, race records and Celine. No wonder, then, that shortly thereafter he states that "a good artist is a deadly enemy of society; and the most dangerous thing that can happen to an enemy, no matter how cynical, is to become a beneficiary" (355). This essentially revolutionary attitude is a result of his belief that "I 'conceive of' my work as an effort to be faithful to my perceptions" (356), and any efforts to conform to a usable past or previous artistic models would necessarily mean a falsification of those perceptions.

On the whole, this section, like "Colon," is dominated by anger and fury; and this seems to derive from the awareness that almost any literary undertaking will involve a betrayal of reality and that this betrayal is taking place constantly and in all areas. In relation to the work as a whole, this attitude is merely an outgrowth of the preoccupation with the problem of how to be true to the specific experience and at the same time find a way to make the communication of that experience a valid experience for the reader.

The fourth large section of the book ("Part Three:

Inductions") is prefaced with the 43d Psalm, "I will go unto the altar of God"; its theme, symmetrically related to that of the second section ("A Country Letter"), is that of approach, here presented in more specific details. In keeping with the religious motto, the organization is influenced by the Mass:

First
    First meetings
Second
    Gradual
    Reversion
    Introit
Third
    Second Introit
    In the room: the Testament
    In the room: In bed.

The purpose of the section is to show Agee in interaction with the farmers themselves on a personal level that has not really been evident before: in the previous sections the confrontation has taken place primarily on the written page; here, of course, it occurs on the written page *as well as* in the actuality that the written page is trying to approach.

The section is written on Agee's second and third planes of narrative, straight recording "as it happened," now and then interrupted by reconstruction, and a more essayistic treatment of details. Even more interesting, the whole section is written in the form of a letter addressed to the farmers, and what he tries to express in it is his absolute love and compassion for them; thus he tells Mrs. Ricket: ". . . and there was not a thing you could do, nothing, not a word of remonstrance you could make, my dear, my love, my little crazy, terrified child" (364); and later, to Louise: "and it is while I am watching you here, Louise, that suddenly yet very quietly I realize a little more clearly that I am probably going to be in love with you" (369). Later, spending his first night with the Gudgers, he has the feeling that after a long search he has finally come home; yet here, too, he feels the betrayal implied in his different way of life, way of thinking, way of being:

. . . the feeling increased itself upon me that at the end of a wandering and seeking, so long it had begun before I was born, I had apprehended and now sat at rest in my own home, between two who were my brother and sister, yet less that than something else; these, the wife my age exactly, the husband four years older, seemed not other than my own parents, in whose patience I was so different, so diverged, so strange as I was; and all that surrounded me, that silently strove in through my senses and stretched me full, was familiar and dear to me as nothing else on earth, and as if well known in a deep past and long years lost; so that I could wish that all my chance life was in truth the betrayal, the curable delusion, that it seemed, and that this was my right home, right earth, right blood, to which I would never have true right. For half my blood is just this; and half my right of speech; and by bland chance alone is my life so softened and sophisticated in the years of my defenselessness, and I am robbed of a royalty I can not only never claim, but never properly much desire or regret. And so in this quiet introit, and in all the time we have stayed in this house, and in all we have sought, and in each detail of it, there is so keen, sad, and precious a nostalgia as I can scarcely otherwise know; a knowledge of brief truancy into the sources of my life, whereto I have no rightful access, having paid no price beyond love and sorrow. (415)

This passage is remarkable because it echoes, on a personal level, the technical or "aesthetic" problem presented earlier. While betrayal earlier was implicit in the task of trying to communicate the actuality of a certain material, here it seems a betrayal to have abandoned the simple form of life for a "softened" and "sophisticated" life. Yet this sense of betrayal is basically a result of the realization that the more specialized the individual, the more isolated and incommunicable his separate "globe," or, in other words, that because individuals are different ("of all these each is a life, a full universe"—110), full communication is impossible.

This whole section is colored by the love Agee feels for this family, and he constantly confronts the difficulty of being true to his feelings as well as his perceptions:

All this while we are talking some: short of exact recording, which is beyond my memory, I can hardly say how: the forms of these plainest and most casual actions are the hardest I can conceive of to set down straight as they happen; and each is somewhat more beautiful and more valuable, I feel, than, say, the sonnet form. This form was one in which two plain people and one complex one who scarcely know each other discourse while one eats and the others wait for him to finish so they may get back to bed: it has the rhythms and inflections of this triple shyness, of sleepiness, of fast eating, of minds in the influence of lamplight between pine walls, of talk which means little or nothing of itself and much in its inflections: What is the use? What is there I can do about it? (417)

But despite the fact that his perceptions and their consequent emotions constantly exceed his ability to communicate, there is happiness in discovering a new world: "I don't exactly know why anyone should be 'happy' under these circumstances, but there's no use laboring the point: I was: outside the vermin, my senses were taking in nothing but a deep-night, unmeditatable consciousness of a world which was newly touched and beautiful to me" (427–28). To discover a world "newly touched and beautiful" is, to speak metaphorically, the predicament of Adam, and it is the first and most essential approach to reality, in human terms (rather than in those of science or, for that matter, art).

Thus, this section brings to a preliminary close the movement which has been evident throughout the book. The effort to approach reality, "to recognize the stature of a portion of unimagined existence," leads to the discovery of a world. The personal quest for the reality of certain actual lives leads to a discovery of love and a home and parents. And as the approach began, in "A Country Letter," with a dawn scene in which the family prepares for the day, so in "Inductions" night is fallen again and the family prepares for bed: we have come full circle and are back where we started—with a difference.

Just as the first section of the book serves to prepare us for what is coming in the future, so the last, the fifth section, serves to sum up, to conclude. As the first section begins in the primeval night before creation, so "Shady Grove," the picture of a country churchyard, is the final and inevitable farewell: "soon, quite soon now, in two years, in five, in forty, it will all be over, and one by one we shall all be drawn into the planet beside one another; let us then hope better of our children, and of our children's children" (439). This farewell leads naturally into a graveside prayer: "in the teeth of all hope of cure which shall pretend its denial and hope of good use to men, let us most quietly and in most reverent fierceness say, not by its captive but by its utmost meanings: Our father, who art in heaven . . ." (439).

That prayer is the end of the book proper: what follows are explanations and comments. First, two images of Squinchy Gudger and Ellen Woods, which, with strongly sexual imagery, manage to suggest, microcosmically, the vitality and flowering of human divinity. Then follows the title statement from Ecclesiasticus: the important part is the conclusion, which gives an ironic and compassionate twist to the title of the book:

And some there be which have no memorial; who perished, as though they had never been; and are become as though they had never been born; and their children after them.

But these were merciful men, whose righteousness hath not been forgotten.

With their seed shall continually remain a good inheritance, and their children are within the covenant.

Their seed standeth fast, and their children for their sakes. Their seed shall remain for ever, and their glory shall not be blotted out.

Their bodies are buried in peace; but their name liveth for evermore.

The "Notes and Appendices" that follow assemble all sorts of comments on the undertaking: first, a list of suggested study material which includes not only Southern novelists and Walker Evans's photographs but race-records as well; second, a newspaper clipping declaring that "Beethoven cannot disturb the peace": considering Agee's view of the artist as a deadly enemy to society, this is a highly ironic commentary; third, an article on Margaret Bourke-White which seems to indicate her disastrous inability to understand what reality is and how it is to be captured by the camera; fourth, a definition of tenant farmers and "sharecroppers," carefully pointing out various ways and reasons these words are misused, and appending, for emphasis, a gigantic list of "other anglosaxon monosyllables:" this list, including words from "god" through "john-ford" and "howdoyoufeelnow" to "defense," appears almost meaningless but is simply an attempt to show that nearly all words can be, and are, constantly misused, and that an investigation of the "sharecropping" problem really should begin with a purification of language in order to establish communication; fifth, a list of Blake's aphorisms from *The Marriage of Heaven and Hell*, all exemplifying Blake's basically dynamic attitude toward the universe: "Everything that is is holy." On the whole, these comments are a convenient way of summarizing attitudes and opinions consonant with the work as a whole which would take long chapters to explain in full.

Then the book is brought to its close by the last section of *On the Porch*. Experiencing the "frightening joy of hearing the world talk to itself" (469) in the sound of foxes calling to each other, Agee is brought to realize not only that "communication of such a thing is not only beyond possibility but irrelevant to it" (469) but also that

in love the restraint in focus and the arrest and perpetuation of joy seems entirely possible and simple, and its failure inexcusable, even while we know it is beyond the power of all biology and even while, like the fading of flowerlike wonder out of a breast to which we are becoming habituated, that exquisite joy lies, fainting through change upon change, in the less and less prescient palm of the less and less godlike, more and more steadily stupefied, human, ordinary hand. (469-70)

Thus, even the failure of love to renew itself is accepted as a human failure, and Agee finds himself "thinking, analyzing, remembering, in the human and artist's sense praying, chiefly over matters of the present and of that immediate past which was a part of the present" (471). And that prayer is as close as anyone can come to reality.

Even a lengthy discussion of *Let Us Now Praise Famous Men*, such as this one, cannot fully explore all the complexities of this highly intricate work. But it should be clear by now that the book is by no means only an "extraordinary grab bag" or some beautiful photographs accompanied by some overly long self-centered prose poetry. The book has a logical and carefully designed structure which, in fact, approaches the kind of symmetry and simpleness Agee sees in the Gudger house.

This symmetry and simplicity is also the basic characteristic of Walker Evans's photographs. In the introduction, Agee points out that "the photographs are not illustrative. They, and the text, are coequal, mutually independent, and fully collaborative" (xv). It seems at first difficult to say anything about the pictures exactly because they are so devoid of artifice. They approach their subjects squarely, with maximum honesty, trying above all to let the world speak for itself without the kind of emotional effects imposed by a photographer like Margaret Bourke-White as she appears in the reprinted interview in the book. And just as Agee recognizes that his basic experience is altered by the simple act of writing about it, so Evans recognizes that a subject facing the camera will necessarily be influenced by this very fact. The vast majority of the portraits are, therefore, straightforwardly posed: it is possible to sense in the subjects themselves their embarrassment, their suspicion and guarded reserve in front of the strange camera eye; and these reactions become part of the subject matter. Similarly, the pictures of the farm houses avoid the contrived camera angles and elaborate compositions that might create a dynamic vitality which is not originally present in the houses themselves. Instead, these are seen as squarely placed on the ground, as houses rather than subject matter for artistic photography. The pictures are mercilessly developed to show the texture of things, not in order to compare its beauty to something else but to let it speak for itself. The beauty of these pictures is, thus, not in the subject matter, which is often ugly or sordid, or in what the photographer does with it, but simply in the artless perception of stark, honest truth. As such, they are a challenge to the reader's eye in much the same way that Agee's text challenges his mind.

Despite almost forbidding originality, it is well to remember that *Let Us Now Praise Famous Men* grew out of the Depression and the thirties in general. (That it was not published until 1941 only adds, in a superficial sense, to its originality.) In one section of the book, written in 1937, Agee confesses that "I am a Communist by sympathy and conviction" (249). Later, in 1939, he tells *Partisan Review* that he has "felt forms of allegiance or part-allegiance to catholicism and to the communist party . . . I am most certainly 'for' an 'intelligent' 'communism'; no other form or theory of government seems to me conceivable; but even this is only a part of much more, and a means to an end" (355-56). Communism in the thirties was not just a political party one might choose depending on individual political philosophy; it was part of a much larger call for action that went up in many areas in the wake of the Depression. This emphasis on action even infiltrated the world of art: as Harold Rosenberg has put it, "the mixing of art with action philosophies had from the twenties forward become a major innovating factor in literature (Social Realism, Existentialism), as in painting (Action Painting) and on the stage (the Theatre of the Absurd)." [36] In writing *Let Us Now Praise Famous Men*, Agee certainly

conceived of it as a call to action, but he was also intelligent enough to see that it would have to be something
more than the descriptive propaganda afforded by Social
Realism in general which could be comfortably read in the
living room and reduced to literary clichés, judgments on
style, and comments on the "shocking" subject matter.
What he aimed for, instead, was a "human effort which
must require human co-operation" (111). This means that
the *only* way to see Agee's work is not as a book about
"sharecropping" but as a book about the writing of a book
about "sharecropping," and this, in turn, means that what
the reader is experiencing is not the ordinary fictionalized
(or psuedo-fictionalized) account of reality but the writer's
performance of an action or gesture in words as a response
to an *actual* human situation.

This action or gesture cannot easily be defined in ordinary terms: its complete definition is, of course, the book
itself. But casting around for suitable metaphors, one is
perhaps most arrested by the idea that the book as a whole
is a prayer. Martin Buber has suggested a definition of
prayer which may be useful in this context:

We call prayer in the pregnant sense of the term that speech
of man to God which, whatever else is asked, ultimately asks
for the manifestation of the divine Presence, for this Presence's
becoming dialogically perceivable. The single presupposition
of a genuine state of prayer is thus the readiness of the whole
man for this Presence, simple turned-towardness, unreserved
spontaneity.[37]

This "simple turned-towardness" is, of course, essentially
an exercise in perceiving reality as it is, be it metaphysical
or secular. In the book, the momentum of Agee's undertaking takes him from the simple fury of recording the
abuse of the universe on the lives of certain people to the

complex acceptance of this reality simply because, as reality, it must be accepted for what it is before anything can be done about it. Thus, the modified joy and happiness of the final section of the book is the result not of a placid acceptance of a social abuse but of the realization that even human misery and failure must be affirmed as part of life itself before these miseries can even be perceived clearly. In that sense, the whole book is simply a hymn to praise the glory of God.

Erik Wensberg has pointed to the stylistic relationship between Agee's prose and the Bible.[38] Metaphorically speaking, one might even go further and suggest that *Let Us Now Praise Famous Men* is a "biblical" book, for its peculiar character derives not from its qualities as a description of certain events, persons, and places, but from its characteristics as an instance of revealed truth. While it is common to study (and even appreciate) the Bible as literature, it is obvious that the primary impact of such a work is due to its implicit assertion that its content is *actual* truth (and not just "truth" within the boundaries of fiction, requiring the customary suspension of disbelief). In other words, this is a truth which exists *a priori* to the work of art; and the artist has the courage (or faith) to assert that there exists an inevitable relationship between life and art: no matter how unified and organically structured the work of art, its primary quality must be that it deals with a living human situation. In that sense, any good work of art is a prayer straddling the customary gap between "art" and "life"; and it is in that realization, finally, that Agee and Evans, at the conclusion of their work, lie "thinking, analyzing, remembering, in the human and artist's sense praying, chiefly over matters of the present and of that immediate past which was a part of the present."

III

SAD DAY, INDEED

FILM CRITICISM

*One foresees the sad day, indeed,
when Agee on Films will be the
subject of a Ph.D. thesis.*

W. H. Auden

James Agee grew up with the movies, and his interest in the new art form was early and long-lasting. Whatever its value as a biographical document, one remembers the introductory scene in *A Death in the Family* with Jay and the six-year-old Rufus at the movies watching "William S. Hart with both guns blazing and his long, horse face and his long, hard lip" and Charlie Chaplin "squattily walking with his toes out and his knees wide apart, as if he were chafed." [1] At Exeter, Agee wrote a letter to Father Flye which indicated his awareness of the dismal quality of most movies and at the same time his willingness to look for surprises: "Have you read *Sorrell and Son*? I haven't, but I saw (don't laugh) an excellent movie made of it." [2] A few years later, while at Harvard, Agee started corresponding with Dwight Macdonald, mostly about movies.

Already at this time he entertained notions of being a movie director; he wrote to Macdonald about a project with a friend: "The idea is that I'll devise shots, angles, camera work, etc., and stories; he'll take care of the photography and lighting." [3] His tastes at this time, Macdonald writes, seem to have conformed to those of young movie enthusiasts: "We both admired the standard things—Griffith, Chaplin, Stroheim, the Russians, the Germans—despised the big American productions ('*Noah's Ark* is the worst and most pretentious movie ever made,' he wrote) and looked desperately for signs of life in Hollywood." [4] In the long poem called "Dedication," Agee included Charlie Chaplin among those "living and soon to die who tell truth or tell of truth, or who honorably seek to tell, or who tell the truths of others." [5]

During this period, the mid-thirties, he also had some interesting comments on movies in letters to Father Flye. In October 1934, for instance, he wrote: "Do you ever happen to see any of the Silly Symphonies by Walt Disney? On the whole they are very beautiful. A sort of combination of Mozart, super-ballet, and La Fontaine." [6] Another comment, two years later, shows the same kind of perception of essentials: "Saw the new Charlie Chaplin a while back . . . it's a wonderful thing to see—a lot, to me, as if Beethoven were living now and had completed another symphony." [7] Finally, it is worth pointing out that Agee's appreciation of the moving pictures is related to his admiration for the art of photography as such: in *Let Us Now Praise Famous Men*, he points out that the camera, if it is handled "cleanly and literally in its own terms," is "like the phonograph record and like scientific instruments and unlike any other leverage of art, incapable of recording anything but absolute, dry truth." [8]

In 1941, Agee began to review movies, anonymously, for *Time;* in 1942, he began writing a personal movie column for *The Nation*; both jobs ended in 1948. After that he wrote a number of feature articles on films (for *Life* and other magazines), before he began devoting more of his time to Hollywood and television work.

Only two years after Agee had begun writing for *The Nation*, W. H. Auden wrote a remarkably appreciative letter to the editors of that journal. Although Auden's praise is perhaps slightly marred by his admission that "I do not care for movies very much and I rarely see them," his appraisal reflects the kind of personal appeal that Agee's reviews seem to have had to many readers:

In my opinion, his column is the most remarkable regular event in American journalism today. What he says is of such profound interest, expressed with such extraordinary wit and felicity, and so transcends its ostensible—to me, rather unimportant—subject that his articles belong in that very select class—the music critiques of Berlioz and Shaw are the only other members I know—of newspaper work which has permanent literary value.[9]

When Agee died in 1955, his reputation as a film critic had grown to such an extent that most reviewers of *Agee on Film: Reviews and Comments*, published in 1958, either simply asserted his absolute greatness in the field or took the opposite side and tried to modify their praise to show that he was not all *that* remarkable. Arthur Knight, for example, came right out and called him "the best movie critic this country has ever had." [10] Gerald Weales echoed him in *Reporter* by calling the book "America's most important contribution to film criticism." Weales pointed, in particular, to Agee's "casual, unselfconscious" use of "the word 'poem' to describe a film in which realism is lifted beyond itself into the aesthetic," and he also thought that Agee's "descriptions of the photographic texture of films and his recognition of the ways the textures were used or misused are easily the most perceptive accounts of pure 'seeing' that film criticism offers." [11]

Jonathan Harker, in *Film Quarterly*, admitted that "Agee's judgment is not impeccable, seen with the hindsight of ten to fifteen years; it is only incomparably the best of his period"; the most admirable quality of the criticism, he found, was that "Agee's respect for films, for their creators, for their audiences, and for himself, is everywhere evident; this sensitivity to the point of embarrassment, evident in his fiction, gives his film criticism a modesty, decency, and distinction which are pretty well extinct." [12] This sensitivity led, as Arlene Croce pointed out, to a moral stand: "His understandings of what films were and of what they could become was such that he was capable of genuine moral evulsion where others saw only the stupidity perpetrated (naturally) by an inferior medium." [13] In a similar vein, Richard Griffith, pointing out that the columns in *The Nation* were "an almost naked personal expression," remarked that "it is sometimes hard to keep in mind that his monotonous denunciations of purblind Hollywood spring from a love for the movie medium so fierce as to make him want to remold it nearer to his heart's desire with his own hands." [14]

Of the slightly more critical reviewers, most concentrated on Agee's passion for truth and integrity, and, with some exceptions, on his ability to put his thoughts into words: Bosley Crowther, for instance, promoted for the occasion from the *New York Times* to *American Scholar*, said that "Agee's distinction as a critic was his exceptional sensitivity to the intimate nature of cinema expression and his ability to put his feelings into vivid, terse, and witty words." [15] While being annoyed and bored by the length of the volume, Winfield T. Scott blamed this on the editing and pointed out that "as a movie critic, and probably in any role, Agee had a fine mixture of spiritual warmth and intellectual acerbity. In all the arts he was angry for truth, for honesty, and integrity; and found little of it, and little that was not compromised." [16] Stanley Kauffmann, too, thought the volume should have been more carefully edited; and although he disagreed with many of Agee's judgments he thought Agee's greatest asset was his passion: the impression he got from the reviews was that of "a man of sensibility and mind putting every nerve and brain-cell, every memory and hope, completely at the disposal of a major contemporary art." [17]

Norman Holland, writing in *Hudson Review*, found Agee "witty, intelligent, and overpoweringly sincere, but, with only a handful of exceptions, his reviews say no more than run-of-the-mill newspaper commentaries." Besides, he thought, "Agee tends (like most critics of today) to over-rate the silent era by confusing final artistic merit with the mere invention of visual technique." [18] Finally, the author of an anonymous note in *The New Yorker* seemed to find only deplorable excesses in the volume:

Perhaps the most striking thing about the book is Agee's unquenchable love of his subject, a condition that, though it is the cornerstone of any true criticism, repeatedly pushes him into some notable excesses—tiresome, embattled attacks against the softness and stupidity of Hollywood; near-fawning pieces on D. W. Griffith and John Huston; stilted and rather tasteless wisecracks; revelations of self that, though invariably arresting, continually get in the way of his subject; and, surprisingly, some bad writing, in which adjectives, long sentences, and plain verbal fury become, here and there, unintelligible stews.[19]

Still, even this reviewer was forced to concede that "the result is some of the best, if shaggiest, film criticism yet written in this country." [20]

Perhaps the single most famous piece of Agee's film criticism is the essay, "Comedy's Greatest Era," which appeared in *Life*, September 3, 1949. In many ways, this essay is representative of Agee's work as a critic. For one thing, it is a relatively sustained piece of writing in contrast to the rather rambling comments of the weekly columns in *The Nation*. On the other hand, in its use of the *Time-Life* idiom, or what has been called Luce-talk, the essay differs from the very individual expression of the weekly columns. Still, it is worth remembering that in a very real sense Agee did *choose* to work for the Luce empire and that he did choose to present his essay in *Life*. Whatever the damages wrought by such circumstances on Agee's style, the work itself, regarded for its own sake, stands as an expression of the totality of the writer's experience and choices; and to glean pearls of cinematic insight from Agee's essay, all the while complaining of the vast field of cliché-ridden journalism, is as unsound as complaining that Faulkner's novels are not more like Dickens's. "Comedy's Greatest Era" is, finally, representative of the kind of work Agee chose to do, and a brief analysis will reveal both Agee's achievements and his shortcomings as a critic.

The essay has a striking enough introduction:

In the language of screen comedians four of the main grades of laugh are the titter, the yowl, the bellylaugh and the boffo.

The titter is just a titter. The yowl is a runaway titter. Anyone who has ever had the pleasure knows all about a belly-laugh. The boffo is the laugh that kills. An ideally good gag, perfectly constructed and played, would bring the victim up this ladder of laughs by cruelly controlled degrees to the top rung, and would then proceed to wobble, shake, wave and brandish the ladder until he groaned for mercy. Then, after the shortest possible time out for recuperation, he would feel the first wicked tickling of the comedian's whip once more and start up a new ladder. (2)*

This is arresting, witty, and elegant. In beginning the paragraph with the contrast between academic definitions ("In the language of screen comedians four of the main grades of laugh are . . .") and the simple straightforward terms to be explained, Agee manages to suggest the contrast between "nice" and "vulgar," which is another theme of the essay:

"Nice" people, who shunned all movies in the early days, condemned the Sennett comedies as vulgar and naïve. But millions of less pretentious people loved their sincerity and sweetness, their wild-animal innocence and glorious vitality. They could not put these feelings into words, but they flocked to the silents. The reader who gets back deep enough into that world will probably even remember the theater: the barefaced honky-tonk and the waltzes by Waldteufel, slammed out on a mechanical piano; the searing redolence of peanuts and demirep perfumery, tobacco, and feet and sweat; the laughter of unrespectable people having a hell of a fine time, laughter as violent and steady and deafening as standing under a waterfall. (6–7)

Even as he explains it, the careless grammar of the dangling verbal in the last sentence is "unrespectable" enough to sug-

* Page numbers in parentheses refer, in this chapter, to *Agee on Film: Reviews and Comments* (McDowell, Obolensky, 1958)

gest which side the writer is on. In the same vein, the first paragraph presents a definition that is not a definition: "the titter is just a titter"; and its inadequacy as definition is more than outweighed by the tacit suggestion that everybody knows what it means, anyway, and that this is the way "unrespectable" people respond when pedants insist on a definition of terms. The second definition is not much better, as it refers back to the first: "The yowl is a runaway titter." The third is likewise self-evident: "Anyone who has ever had the pleasure knows all about a bellylaugh." The fourth definition, finally, approaches normal logical standards: "The boffo is the laugh that kills." Thus, in a parody on academic definitions of terms, these four sentences succeed only in giving names to four undefined grades of laughter, suggesting, however, that these grades are physically so easily recognizable that they do not have to be defined at all. This "physical" pseudo-definition of laughter is continued in the rest of the paragraph, which, with images drawn from an almost perverted form of torture, describes the paradoxical pleasure of absolute physical exhaustion from too much laughter.

As description, and as introduction to a popular essay, this paragraph achieves its results economically and effectively. What is even more interesting, however, is that it actually provides the critical assumptions underlying the essay as a whole. In comparing modern screen comedy with the silents, Agee measures their qualities simply in terms of laughter:

The reader can get a fair enough idea of the current state of screen comedy by asking himself how long it has been since he has had that treatment. The best of comedies these days hand out plenty of titters and once in a while it is possible to achieve a yowl without overstraining. . . . As for those happy atavists who remember silent comedy in its heyday and the bellylaughs and boffos that went with it, they have something close to an absolute standard by which to measure the deterioration. (2–3)

Later, in his discussion of Harold Lloyd, Agee makes a similar suggestion: "If great comedy must involve something beyond laughter, Lloyd was not a great comedian. If plain laughter is any criterion—and it is a healthy counterbalance to the other—few people have equaled him, and nobody has ever beaten him" (12).

In assuming laughter as a criterion of quality in a comedy, Agee is following to its logical extreme the observation that in silent-screen comedy, unlike "literary" comedy, there are no words. More like farce in this respect, it depends, therefore, not primarily on character but on types and, above all, on action. In determining exactly what situations are funny, Agee depends to a certain extent on traditional criteria. For instance, he gives a splendid example of the humorous effect of the unexpected absurdity: "Laurel and Hardy are trying to move a piano across a narrow suspension bridge. The bridge is slung over a sickening chasm, between a couple of Alps. Midway they meet a gorilla" (8). The logic of this kind of situation is of the paradoxical variety, which sooner or later leads into an unpredictable absurdity (and Agee himself later points out that humor is "ruthlessly logical" —18). Another example is the image of Buster Keaton wearing his "deadly horizontal hat . . . standing erect at the prow as his little boat is being launched. The boat goes grandly down the skids and, just as grandly, straight on to the bottom. Keaton never budges. The last you see of him, the water lifts the hat off the stoic head and it floats away" (15). Keaton provides several examples for Agee of this type of gag: "Trapped in the side-wheel of a ferryboat, saving himself from drowning only by walking, then desperately running, inside the accelerating wheel like a squirrel in a cage, his only real concern was, obviously, to keep his hat on" (16). In discussing Harold Lloyd, Agee also points out that the ultrapredictable can be just as funny as the unexpected:

As Lloyd approaches the end of his horrible hegira up the side of the building in *Safety Last*, it becomes clear to the audience, but not to him, that if he raises his head another couple of inches, he is going to get murderously conked by one of the four arms of a revolving wind gauge. He delays the evil moment almost interminably, with one distraction and another, and every delay is a suspense-tightening laugh; he also gets his foot nicely entangled in a rope, so that when he does get hit, the payoff of one gag sends him careening head downward through the abyss into another. (11–12)

In a very real sense, it is more difficult to analyze a play of action than a play of words. The words in a play, after all, stand as something concrete which can be examined time after time, whereas, in a film, there is no notation for the action. It must first be described; only then can analysis commence. The validity of the analysis comes therefore to depend on the validity of the description. This description, in turn, depends on the proper perception of action as form. Now, the silent-screen comedy has one of the simplest and most easily recognizable of forms, and its slow build-up of increasingly ludicrous incidents to a final climactic chase is obvious to every viewer. What is remarkable in Agee's perception of form is his ability to recognize the nuances as well as the larger implications of this form. Thus, in the beginning of the essay he describes a typical silent sight-gag:

When a silent comedian got hit on the head he seldom let it go so flatly. He realized a broad license, and a ruthless discipline within that license. It was his business to be as funny as possible physically, without the help or hindrance of words. So he gave us a figure of speech, or rather of vision, for loss of consciousness. In other words he gave us a poem, a kind of poem, moreover, that everybody understands. (3)

Such gags are "fine clichés from the language of silent comedy in its infancy" (3), and the best of the silent comedians were successful, because, in essence, they were "deep conservative classicists" (3) who did not try to break away from the established idiom and who, "like the masters, . . . knew, and sweated to obey, the laws of their craft" (19). The mark of genius in a comedian was his ability to achieve subtle variations on the basic idiom: "Most of the time, however, Chaplin got his laughter less from the gags, or from milking them in any ordinary sense, than through his genius for what may be called *inflection*— the perfect, changeful shading of his physical and emotional attitude toward the gag" (9). Harold Lloyd could achieve the same kind of variation; in *Safety Last*, most of which takes place along the face of a skyscraper, "each new floor is like a new stanza in a poem; and the higher and more horrifying it gets, the funnier it gets" (11). Likewise, "much of the charm and edge of Keaton's comedy . . . lay in the subtle leverages of expression he could work against his nominal dead pan" (16). To Agee, the act of throwing a pie was not a simple routine but a gag capable of infinite variations; describing a Laurel and

Hardy two-reeler almost exclusively devoted to pie-throwing, he writes:

The first pies were thrown thoughtfully, almost philosophically. Then innocent bystanders began to get caught into the vortex. At full pitch it was Armageddon. But everything was calculated so nicely that until late in the picture, when havoc took over, every pie made its special kind of point and piled on its special kind of laugh. (6)

In the end, however, Agee's perception of form and his communication of it retain a strong element of subjectivity. As there are no words that can be defined, discussed and analyzed before they are evaluated, but only the naked perception of the individual eye (which, of course, has such rich capabilities to perceive shades of form that they simply cannot be discussed in the really limited vocabulary employed in semantics and literary analysis), it is the individual mind which selects how to limit its impressions for purposes of discussion and description. The immediacy of the picture loses some of its force in the reconciliation with words, and, one way or another, criticism must come to terms with that loss. This is not to say that all film criticism is tinged with subjectivity to such a degree that it is useless, but simply that the critic must arrive at his judgments in the face of possible charges of subjectivity. This seems to account for the common split in film criticism between the "literary critics" who pay attention solely to content and words because there exists already a useful vocabulary which can be applied, and the "film" enthusiasts who discuss the rhythms and motions of the camera in such detail that content seems finally irrelevant.

In "Comedy's Greatest Era," Agee solves this problem

by relying on, instead of avoiding, his own subjectivity: in other words, instead of obtaining a limited objectivity at the expense of the material, he assumes an attitude of conscious subjectivity which permits him to give a total response, in human terms, to the material. This response can be traced even outside the essay itself; for Agee did not choose to write it as a "scholarly," "critical" essay, but as a feature article for *Life* (whether or not as a result of financial necessity is, in the final analysis, irrelevant). Without resorting to the outspoken subjectivity of the first person singular, the essay presents a personal response to the golden era of silent comedy. This is evident in the organization and in the style, idiom, and metaphors of the essay. For one thing, the use of laughter as a criterion for comedy, as well as the difficulty of analyzing in words the action of these films, leads to an emphasis on description; and style is used as a supportive means to prove that what is said to be funny really *is* funny. For instance, after the description of Laurel and Hardy trying to move a piano over a narrow suspension bridge, the next sentence, "Midway they meet a gorilla," echoes in its brevity and objectivity as flat statement the ruthlessly detached logic which Agee claims is an integral part of silent comedy.

Metaphors and similes render effectively Agee's sensitive impressions: Ben Turpin's "Adam's apple, an orange in a Christmas stocking, pumped with noble emotion" (5); a Sennett comedy chase "built up such majestic trajectory of pure anarchic motion that bathing girls, cops, comics, dogs, cats, babies, automobiles, locomotives, innocent bystanders, sometimes what seemed like a whole city, an entire civilization, were hauled along head over heels in the wake of that energy like dry leaves following an express train" (6); Harold Lloyd looked "like the sort of eager young man who might have quit divinity school to hustle brushes" (8); in Lloyd's *Safety Last*, "the local pigeons treat him like a cross between a lunch wagon and St. Francis of Assisi" (11); Harry Langdon looked "as if he wore diapers under his pants" (13); and, finally, in describing Buster Keaton, Agee uses a mass of metaphors and similes to build up a character:

No other comedian could do as much with the dead pan. He used his great, sad motionless face to suggest various related things: a one-track mind near the track's end of pure insanity; mulish imperturbability under the wildest of circumstances; how dead a human being can get and still be alive; an awe-inspiring sort of patience and power to endure, proper to granite but uncanny in flesh and blood. Everything that he was and did bore out this rigid face and played laughs against it. When he moved his eyes, it was like seeing them move in a statue. His short-legged body was all sudden, machine-like angles, governed by a daft aplomb. When he swept a sema-phorelike arm to point, you could almost hear the electrical impulse in the signal block. When he ran from a cop his transitions from accelerating walk to easy jogtrot to brisk canter to headlong gallop to flogged-piston sprint—always floating, above this frenzy, the untroubled, untouchable face—were as distinct and as soberly in order as an automatic gearshift. (15)

This passage conveys the essentials of the Keaton character admirably and is amusing as well, but our amusement is due here to the description rather than to the character himself. In fact, the passage is just as amusing for those who have seen and appreciated Keaton as for those who have not. The eyes moving in the statue, the electrical impulse in the signal block, the transitions "as distinct and as soberly in order as an automatic gearshift," these are Agee's impressions and the only means at his disposal for conveying in words the wordless actions on the screen.

Adverbs and adjectives are used for this same purpose, in a way that transcends the limitations of the usual Luce-style of writing: "a profusion of hearty young women in disconcerting bathing suits, frisking around with a gaggle of insanely incompetent policemen and of equally certifiable male civilians sporting museum-piece mustaches" (5). This, to be sure, is not the real thing, but the contrast between qualifier and the thing qualified (how can a bathing suit be "disconcerting?"; policemen are symbols of authority and therefore not normally incompetent, much less insanely so; nor do they usually appear in "gaggles") introduces an ironic absurdity which in its own linguistic way imitates the nature and tone of Sennett's slapsticks. It is an example of the same technique when Agee writes that the silent comedians made "ferociously emphatic" gestures (5), wore "agonizingly elaborate drawers" (5), appeared in sets with "megalomaniacally scrolled iron beds" (5), dressed in "tigerish pajamas" (6). Chaplin could portray "the delicately weird mental processes of a man ethereally sozzled" (9), or "probably pantomime Bryce's *The American Commonwealth* without ever blurring a syllable and make it paralyzingly funny into the bargain" (10); Harold Lloyd's unaccepted college boy could win the Big Game "by desperate courage and inspired ineptitude" (10–11); and Buster Keaton's pictures were "like a transcendent juggling act in which it seems that the whole universe is in exquisite flying motion and the one point of repose is the juggler's effortless, uninterested face" (15).

Thus, "Comedy's Greatest Era" is, as criticism, descriptive, impressionistic, evocative, and personal rather than analytic and objective. This is also indicated by the response to its appearance; as the editor of *Agee on Film*, I, points out, "the surprising element was the reaction from people who could have seen few, if any, of the silent comedies, simply because they were too young. The article makes it possible for everyone to be nostalgic for something that perhaps they have never known" (2). In fact, the vitality of the essay is Agee's more than that of the subject matter (which is not to say that the subject matter lacked vitality); this is true of almost all of Agee's film criticism, and it explains why it is still possible to read with great interest those columns in *The Nation* which deal almost exclusively with bad pictures and the reasons for their badness.

In his first review for *The Nation*, on December 26, 1942, Agee tried to outline some of his ambitions as a critic; among other things he wrote:

As an amateur, then, I must as well as I can simultaneously recognize my own ignorance and feel no apology for what my eyes tell me as I watch any given screen, where the proof is caught irrelevant to excuse, and available in proportion to the eye which sees it, and the mind which uses it. (23)

Eight years later, in a *Life* article on John Huston, he outlined, in similar terms, a standard of excellence in movies:

Most movies are made in the evident assumption that the audience is passive and wants to remain passive; every effort is made to do all the work—the seeing, the explaining, the understanding, even the feeling. Huston is one of the few movie artists who, without thinking twice about it, honors his audience. His pictures are not acts of seduction or of benign enslavement but of liberation, and they require, of anyone who enjoys them, the responsibilities of liberty. They continually open the eye and require it to work vigorously; and through the eye they awaken curiosity and intelligence. That, by any virile standard, is essential to good entertainment. It is unquestionably essential to good art. (330)

This emphasis on the visual excitement of movies is not just an awareness of the medium as such but also a realization that the medium is so often abused, both by filmmakers and by audiences. Thus, in the same breath that he asserts the one rule for movies that he cares about, "that the film interest the eyes, and do its job through the eyes," he also points out "that few movie-makers do that, few even of those who are generally well esteemed" (305). For it is not a simple matter of setting up a camera and letting it roll; as always in art, it is a matter of selecting and choosing a viewpoint. Yet, too often this selection manages to falsify the object and to obscure its inherent beauty and power; and it is in contrast to such failures that Agee praises Frank Capra's *Prelude to War* because "there is an eye for the unprecedented powers which can reside in simple record photographs—the ferocious inadvertent caricature, the moment when a street becomes tragic rather than a mere street, the intricate human and political evidence in unknown faces" (40). The truly creative eye "makes a subject be itself with the intensity of a diamond" (33). Unfortunately, the general audience is often so passive that Agee warns his readers to see Jean Vigo's pictures only "if your eye is already sufficiently open so that you don't fiercely resent an artist who tries to open it somewhat wider" (262). And in his brilliant review of Chaplin's *Monsieur Verdoux*, he points out how mistaken the critics are who complained about Chaplin's lack of new techniques and visual excitement:

To be sure, you have to be competent to see what he puts
before you; and thanks to the depravities of the latter-day
"style," most of us have spoiled eyes. We cannot appreciate
swiftness and uninsistence; nor the bracing absence of fancy
composition and prettiness; nor Chaplin's genius for "mood"
when that is important (the first great shot of Verdoux's
closed garden); nor the atmosphere, authenticity, and beauty
in mock formlessness (some wonderful loose group shots, full
of glass, gravel, gray sky, pale heads, and dark clothing, at the
garden party); nor for visual wit (the astoundingly funny
long shot of the lake, with the murder boat almost impercep-
tibly small). We are just smart enough to recognize a cliché;
never enough to see how brilliantly a master can use it.   (255)

The attitude underlying this insistence on the function
of the naked eye is a deep respect for human reality as it
is: any "artistic" treatment of the material must be undertaken not for the glory of the art or the artist but for the
glory of the reality itself. In praising the "re-enactments"
of films like *Open City* and *The Raider*, Agee suggests
that "they show a livelier aesthetic and moral respect for
reality—which 'realism' can as readily smother as liberate—
than most fictional films, commercial investments in professional reliability, ever manage to" (237). Such respect,
as he finds it in John Huston's war documentary *San Pi-
etro*, for instance, "accepts the facts and treats them as
materials relevant to anger, tenderness, pride, veneration,
and beauty" (164). It shows the "urgency of human beings" (195). It is apparent, although on "a not-quite-real,
smart level" in Billy Wilder's feeling for "the streets and
suffocating marriage hutches and calm-lighted Piggly-Wig-
glies and heartlessly resonant offices of his city" (119) in
Double Indemnity. In *A Tree Grows in Brooklyn*, it is this
kind of respect which makes the streets and tenements "as
lovingly and exhaustively detailed and as solid-looking as

any [sets] I can remember" although they still cannot quite approximate "the real thing, full of its irreducible present tense and its unpredictable proliferations of energy and beauty" (141–42).

Agee's respect for human reality makes it the function of art to picture as accurately and honestly as possible the inherent beauty and immediacy of life. In a neat reversal of the all-too-common demand for "escape" pictures, he even recommends the British war information documentaries "almost with reverence as the finest 'escapes' available" because they present a "decently ventilated and healthful world, where, if only for the duration, human beings are worthy of themselves and of each other" (58). In a deeper sense, this attitude obliterates the distinction between life and art (as Agee explicitly pointed out in *Let Us Now Praise Famous Men*): if it is the glory of art that it presents the "reality" of life, then art is what it is, not as an imitation of nature, or a selection of "real" enough components which give us a picture of what life is like, but because it possesses the very qualities of life itself. The distinction between what the eye observes inside the movie house and what it see outside it is basically false: in both cases, the eye sees a human event, and just as human events have their contexts, so do movies. If, for instance, *Bataan* seems to portray war shallowly, this may be because it is "pure artifice," but as such "its image of war is not only naïve, coarse-grained, primitive; it is also honest, accomplished in terms of its aesthetic, and true" (45). Once the context is recognized, however, both life and art entail a response in human rather than critical terms. In the same sense that morality influences certain aspects of life, it colors art. Thus, the response called for is primarily personal and human rather than objective and critical. This lends to Agee's columns a quite refreshing unprofessional quality. (Agee, of course, would have considered "professional" a dirty word, as when, in *Let Us Now Praise Famous Men*, he states that the authors propose to deal with their subject "not as journalists, sociologists, politicians, entertainers, humanitarians, priests, or artists, but seriously.")[21] In his first column, he calls himself an "amateur" but refuses to apologize for it; and perhaps the most astonishing thing about Agee's eight-year career as a movie critic is that he managed to avoid becoming a professional—"political as well as cinematic" (234)—and remained an amateur in the best sense of the word.

It is the unprofessional qualities in Agee that make it possible for him to appreciate such a wide range of cinematic phenomena and to respond to them in simple, human terms. As in "Comedy's Greatest Era," he sided completely with the unsophisticated audience:[22] reviewing (and, incidentally, perceptively praising as psychological melodrama) *The Curse of the Cat People*, he writes:

The West Times Square audience is probably, for that matter, the finest movie audience in the country (certainly, over and over, it has proved its infinite superiority to the run of the "art-theater" devotees—not to mention, on paper which must brave the mails, the quality and conduct of Modern Art film audiences). (86)

And he allows himself an angry outbreak against all kinds of misunderstanding audiences and critics in reviewing Jean Vigo's films; and although the passage seems perhaps excessively uncharitable and irritable, it sustains, in more ways than one, the personal tone that Agee insisted on in his column:

If you regard all experiment as affectation and all that bewilders you as a calculated personal affront, and if you ask of art chiefly that it be easy to take, you are advised not to waste your time seeing Jean Vigo's *Zero de Conduite* and *L'Atalante*; go on back to sleep, lucky Pierre, between the baker's wife and the well-digger's daughter, if you can squeeze in among the reviewers who have written so contemptuously of Vigo's work. If you regard all experiment as ducky, and all bewilderment as an opportunity to sneer at those who confess their bewilderment, and if you ask of art only that it be outré, I can't silence your shrill hermetic cries, or prevent your rush to the Fifth Avenue Playhouse; I can only hope to God I don't meet you there. (262)

As an unsophisticated or unrespectable amateur, then, Agee took it upon himself to see an incredible number of films. He did not confine himself to only the ambitious and respectable products; but, reporting on *Lassie Come Home*, he could write: "Whether from private remembrance or from the show, I got several reverberations of that strangely pure, half-magical tone which certain books, regardless of their other qualities, have for many children" (54). In *The Story of G. I. Joe*, he finds not only a closing scene which "seems to me a war poem as great and as beautiful as any of Whitman's" but also an "angry, bitter nobility of the intention which is implied behind the whole of it" so that "I cannot suggest my regard for it without using such words as veneration and love" (171-73).

As an amateur, again, Agee also took it upon himself to see and report on war documentaries and Army orientation films. In *Let Us Now Praise Famous Men*, he included his answer to *Partisan Review*'s question, "Have you considered the question of your attitude toward the possible entry of the United States into the next world war? What do you think the responsibilities of writers in general are when and if war comes?" [23] After naming a number of alternatives, Agee suggested he would try to "escape from it by whatever means possible and by the same means continue to do my own work." [24] He added:

I am worst confused between "responsibilities" as a "writer" and as a "human being"; which I would presume are identical, yet which involve constant "inhumanity" even in times of no official war. Or, in other words, I consider myself to have been continuously at war for some years, and can imagine no form of armistice. In that war I feel "responsible." I doubt any other form of war could make me feel more so.[25]

In the beginning of the war, Agee thought of the war documentary as a means of participating in the war, of realizing the immensity of actual combat, and he resented all efforts at propaganda and a glorified falsification:

[*With the Marines at Tarawa*] can be highly recommended to anyone who, like myself, needs to diminish so far as he can, the astronomical abyss which exists between the experienced and the inexperienced in war. The faces of individual marines, at the end, are even more humbling and more instructive than the worst of the records of combat.   (82–83)

Even the realism of war can be given honesty and beauty, and, perceiving this, he wrote, in June 1944, that "in *Attack!* there are morning shots, getting men and matériel ashore in the not quite misty, sober light, which overwhelmed me with their doubleness of beauty, almost sublimity, and their almost fragrant immediacy which made me doubt my right to be aware of the beauty at all" (99). Nine months later, however, he suggested that the vicarious experience and participation of war films were similar to those of pornography:

If at an incurable distance from participation, hopelessly incapable of reactions adequate to the event, we watch men killing each other, we may be quite as profoundly degrading ourselves and, in the process, betraying and separating ourselves the farther from those we are trying to identify ourselves with; nonetheless because we tell ourselves sincerely that we sit in comfort and watch carnage in order to nurture our patriotism, our conscience, our understanding, and our sympathies. (152)

The important thing, here, is not the change of attitude itself, but the struggle to perceive the morality of the whole question of war documentaries; the moral quality of that struggle is itself an example of Agee's desire to live up to his responsibilities as both writer and human being in trying to understand the war as accurately as possible.

Comparable to Agee's interest in war pictures is his remarkable column in *The Nation* in April 1945, in which he described the pictures of Franklin D. Roosevelt taken at Teheran and Yalta and during his report to Congress. Superficially, the column is simply an evaluation of Agee's personal impressions of the recently deceased President from newsreels and other filmed reports. Yet, without ever explicitly referring to the fact, the column suggests that simple, unadorned reality, photographed carefully and with reverence, can bring forth the inner qualities of a man in a way that words and language cannot.

The need for a response in human terms to movies as human realities made his column extremely personal. He did not hesitate to outline at length his own personal qualifications for viewing certain movies; nor did he hesitate to write down angry reactions, or to overpraise. In 1948, he sees himself forced to admit that "Vittorio de Sica's *Shoeshine* and Luigi Zampa's *To Live in Peace* were overrated by nearly everyone, flagrantly including me" (288), but he conscientiously goes on to suggest that this was because both pictures were essentially "made from the heart, and so touched the heart" (288). In matters of style, too, he was unabashedly (and, sometimes, as a number of critics have pointed out, unfortunately) personal: his first view of Lauren Bacall resulted in the comment:

I can hardly look at her, much less listen to her—she has a voice like a chorus by Kid Ory—without getting caught in a dilemma between a low whistle and a bellylaugh. (121)

Another time he suggested that "watching *The White Cliffs of Dover* is like drinking cup after cup of tepid orange pekoe at a rained-out garden party staged by some deep-provincial local of the English-Speaking Union" (94). In reviewing *The Lost Weekend* and suggesting that the physical experience of a hangover had not been sufficiently well presented, he concludes, "I undershtand that liquor interesh: innerish: intereshtsh are rather worried about thish film. Thash tough" (184). Such comments may certainly be considered in bad taste, or at least less than funny, but when the writer in *The New Yorker* complains about "revelations of self that, although invariably arresting, continually get in the way of his subject," [26] he is mistaken, for, in the context of Agee's criticism, the personal style as well as "revelations of self" are unavoidable parts of the human response which, by definition, must be individual.

Norman Holland, in his review of the film criticism, has suggested that "for the most part, Agee operates strictly at the level of gut reaction: I liked or I didn't like," and that "about the only way of rating his visceral criticism is to see how many people have since agreed." [27] While the first part of this statement is true, the second part is valid only if one accepts Eliot's pronouncement that criticism can never be autonomous but is always dependent on the art which it criticizes. In other words, if criticism is regarded as a product existing in a certain relationship to another given product, the work of art, then this relationship can be evaluated in terms of consistency, accuracy, and pertinence. If, on the other hand, criticism is regarded as a human event, a response, in relation to another human event, the work of art, then it is not the accuracy of the relationship, or its pertinence in critical terms, which is important but its qualities as a human event. These qualities are more difficult to evaluate, but if, with the hindsight of fifteen years, we insist on comparing Agee's critical judgments with current critical opinion, we find only a pretty average score that is no true indication of his importance and influence as a film critic.

Even Holland has observed the consistently moral quality of Agee's criticism: "When Agee calls for realism, he really means honesty. This confusion makes his aesthetic vocabulary oddly ethical. Chaplin, for example, he neatly calls a 'saint.' " [28] This "oddly ethical" point of view is, in fact, at the heart of Agee's criticism with its insistence on the uniqueness and sacredness of human reality. As such, it grows out of the call for action in the twenties and thirties, in the arts, in politics, and in the theater,[29] with the reservation that Agee refused to be lured, as were so many others, into propaganda of one sort or another (Communism, Social Realism) but chose to act simply as a human being. Robert Phelps has suggested that this is where Agee's influence was, and that "nothing that Agee wrote in conventional forms . . . expresses his temperament any better, or more memorably than what he managed to do with his film column in *The Nation*." [30] This highly personal, "oddly ethical" point of view is also, as Stanley Kauffmann has indicated, the result of "a man of sensibility and mind putting every nerve and brain cell, every memory and hope, completely at the disposal of a major contemporary art," [31] and it makes Agee's criticism in essence a celebration of reality in all its forms and of the artist's sense of "what, artistically, is more 'real' than the actual and what is less real" (223). This sense, which, as he showed in a different medium in *Let Us Now Praise Famous Men*, breaks down the distinction between life and art, could produce works of art which, in their combination of fiction and reality, would be infinitely more real than the common products in the field: "The films I most eagerly look forward to will not be documentaries but works of pure fiction, played against, and into, and in collaboration with unrehearsed and uninvented reality" (237).

Perhaps the only film in Agee's reviews even to approach this high expectation is George Rouquier's documentary *Farrabique*. Agee places it "in the whole great line of rural art which extends backwards through Van Gogh and Brueghel to the Georgics and to the *Works and Days*," combining as it does "the cold deep-country harshness of Hesiod with a Virgilian tenderness and majesty" (299). He sees it as "a kind of Bible" and, echoing the Bible, suggests that "this picture is not for cultists, but for those who have eyes capable of seeing what is before them, and minds and hearts capable of caring for what they see" (298).

Finally, Rouquier's great achievement is that he has been able to record accurately the poetic vitality of unadorned reality:

He realizes that, scrupulously handled, the camera can do what nothing else in the world can do: can record unaltered reality; and can be made also to perceive, record, and communicate, in full unaltered power, the peculiar kinds of poetic vitality which blaze in every real thing and which are in great degree, inevitably and properly, lost to every other kind of artist except the camera artist. He is utterly faithful to this realization; and it is clear in nearly every shot that he is infinitely more than a mere documentor, that his poetic intelligence is profound, pure, and vigorous; and it is clear many times over that he has the makings, and now and then the achievement, of a major poet. There is not an invented person or thing in the picture, and the re-enactments, and invented incidents, are perfect examples of the discipline of imagination necessary under these difficult circumstances. One could watch the people alone, indefinitely long, for the inference of his handling of them, to realize that moral clearness and probity are indispensable to work of this kind, and to realize with fuller contempt than ever before how consistently in our time so-called simple people, fictional and nonfictional, are consciously and unconsciously insulted and betrayed by artists and by audiences: it seems as if the man is hardly alive, any more, who is fit to look another man in the eye. But this man is; and this is the finest and strongest record of actual people that I have seen. (296–97)

This is more than criticism and praise: it is, in effect, a credo, and it breathes the awareness that no amount of technique will succeed without the realization that "a movie, like any other work of art, must be made for love" (138).

IV

FICTION AND
UNREHEARSED REALITY

FILM SCRIPTS

In the letter Agee wrote to Dwight Macdonald from Harvard, quoted in the preceding chapter, he mentioned his interest in directing movies together with a friend: "The idea is that I'll devise shots, angles, camera work, etc., and stories; he'll take care of the photography and lighting." [1] At about this time, too, in November 1930, he tried to outline his future to Father Flye:

So far as I can tell, I definitely want to write—probably poetry in the main. At any rate, nothing else holds me in the same way. As you know, I had two other interests just as strong a few years ago—music and directing movies of my own authorship. These have slowly been killed off, partly by brute and voluntary force on my part, chiefly by the overcrowding of my wish to write. Each of them occasionally flares up; last spring I was all but ready to quit college and bum to California and trust to luck for the rest. [2]

It was to be another twenty years before Agee got to California, and then it was not as director, but as scriptwriter.

It is regrettable that he never directed a movie: if his criticism and his screenplays are at all indicative, he might have brought something rare and vital to the screen.

When Agee started writing scripts for Hollywood in the late forties, he had been thinking seriously about movies for more than twenty years. He had also written outlines, sketches and treatments for suggested movies, and some of these were published. In 1937, for instance, Horace Gregory published Agee's "Notes for a Moving Picture: The House" in *New Letters in America*. In 1939, in the first issue of a new film quarterly, *Films*, Agee published his notes for a film treatment of a section of André Malraux's novel *Man's Fate*. Shortly after the war, in April 1946, Agee contributed a rough satiric "sketch for a moving picture," called "Dedication Day," to Dwight Macdonald's journal, *Politics*. The year after, in 1947, he wrote the commentary for Helen Levitt's documentary about a young Negro boy in Harlem, *The Quiet One*. Then came the more commercial scripts. Under contract to Huntington Hartford, Agee wrote a script based on Stephen Crane's "The Blue Hotel" in 1948–49; it was never filmed. Then, in the fall of 1950, Agee, together with John Huston, wrote the script for *The African Queen* after C. S. Forester's novel; the film was produced with some success, and Agee's script received an Academy Award nomination, in 1952.

In 1951–52, Agee adapted another of Stephen Crane's short stories, "The Bride Comes to Yellow Sky," for Huntington Hartford; this, too, was filmed, and Agee played a minor role in the film. During this time, he also wrote narration and paraphrased dialogue "for a quite likeable movie, made in the Philippines, about the youth of Genghiz Khan." [3] Then, in the next year, he wrote a series of scripts for television on the life of Lincoln; these were commissioned by the Ford Foundation and produced by *Omnibus*. In 1953, he wrote perhaps his most ambitious script: an original scenario treatment of the life of Paul Gauguin, *Noa Noa*; it has never been produced. The following year, Agee was back to writing commentary and narration for an Italian travel film, *Green Magic*; he also adapted Davis Grubb's novel *The Night of the Hunter* for the screen: under the direction of Charles Laughton, this became a successful film. During this year, also, he worked on an outline for a movie about musicians in Tanglewood, Mass., in cooperation with Howard Taubman, then the *New York Times* music critic; Agee finished drafting the shooting script for this movie in January 1955,[4] and went on to consider a number of prospects, most of which involved scriptwriting. In his last letter to Father Flye, dated May 11, 1955, he outlined a movie idea about elephants, a surrealistic fantasy with strong religious overtones.

The current charge (or myth) that Agee's talents were largely wasted on inferior material must be checked against this list of his achievements in what is so often called an "inferior" medium. In terms of popular success, perhaps only *The African Queen* is worth remembering; in terms of critical success, that film, the Lincoln scripts, *The Night of the Hunter*, and the documentary *The Quiet One* have commanded a certain amount of respect. It is also worth noting that very few scriptwriters, or, for that matter, directors, in Hollywood, receive a critical response at all comparable to what would happen if they worked in the field of literature. (The exception to this rule is provided by a few original critics, such as Manny Farber and Agee himself.) For all their reluctant admission that the cinema is an art form, most literary critics still implicitly sneer at the movies; while they can appreciate a solid piece of crafts-manship in the average novel, the same qualities in a film become a good reason to ignore it.

The years that Agee worked more or less actively with movies produced a rather remarkable number of fine films (although the trend toward either ambitious, "arty" films or big spectacles had already begun): Robert J. Flaherty's *Louisiana Story*, Laurence Olivier's *Hamlet*, and Michael Powell and Emeric Pressburger's *The Red Shoes*, in 1948; Robert Rossen's *All the King's Men*, Clarence Brown's *Intruder in the Dust* (1949); Orson Welles's *Macbeth*, Billy Wilder's *Sunset Boulevard*, John Huston's *The Asphalt Jungle* (1950) and *The Red Badge of Courage* (1951); Chaplin's *Limelight*, Fred Zinnemann's *High Noon* (1952); Alfred Hitchcock's *I Confess* (1953); Jean Renoir's *The Golden Coach*, Luis Bunuel's *The Adventures of Robinson Crusoe*, Elia Kazan's *On the Waterfront* (1954); Welles's *Othello*, Robert Aldrich's *The Big Knife*, Hitchcock's *The Trouble With Harry* (1955).

During these years, the established American directors of what Manny Farber has called "underground films" [5] (the "male action films" of the thirties and forties) were still active: John Ford (*She Wore a Yellow Ribbon, Wagonmaster, Rio Grande, The Quiet Man, The Long Gray Line*, among others), Howard Hawks (*Red River, The Big Sky*), Raoul Walsh (*Silver River*), Anthony Mann (*Winchester 73, Bend of the River, The Naked Spur*), and William Wellman (*Battleground*). Young, ambitious directors were turning out films that were at least interesting and that often had the courage to deal with controversial issues: Edward Dmytryk (*Crossfire, Give Us This Day*), Elia Kazan (*Gentleman's Agreement, East of Eden*), Mark Robson (*Home of the Brave, Bright Victory*), Fred

Zinnemann (*The Search, The Men, Teresa, From Here to Eternity, The Member of the Wedding*), and Laszlo Benedek (*Death of a Salesman, The Wild One*).

Films such as these (and the list is by no means exhaustive) are not necessarily masterpieces, but they are all of them well-made, craftsmanlike products, sometimes merely entertaining, sometimes controversial, sometimes even brilliant. Yet, excepting perhaps Chaplin and Olivier, one may well ask why the critical élite so consistently refused to deal with these directors with the kind of seriousness afforded novelists in similar circumstances. John Ford's position as the Shakespeare of the American West has been largely unnoticed simply because of a pseudo-cultural emphasis on subject matter; it is only in recent years that the *avant-garde* appreciation of the off-beat and of simple, honest melodrama had become a fad which, as Manny Farber angrily puts it, "shows itself in the inevitable little magazine review which finds an affinity between the subject matter of cowboy films and the inner aesthetics of Cinemah." [6]

The charge that Agee wasted his talents on Hollywood must also be answered with a clearsighted analysis of his scripts. Even a superficial glance shows that he hardly wasted himself on inferior materials: to adapt two Stephen Crane stories and to write an original script on Gauguin's life is ambitious enough to be quite respectable. In a deeper sense, however, the question remains: what exactly did he achieve by working for Hollywood? And was it, in the end, worth it? Does his work in the pictures have the same kind of finality and permanence of value as, for instance, *Let Us Now Praise Famous Men* and *A Death in the Family?*

One reason why these questions are difficult to answer

is the very nature of the scenario or the script. The film is a visual medium and (whatever the correct interpretation of this in terms of aesthetics) film criticism must come to terms with these visual characteristics in order to begin to approach its topic. The film script, on the other hand, is a literary form (it exists in words, like any other genre of literature) which demands to be judged in terms of visual characteristics which, in effect, are not there. In other words, the film script is "intentional," and as script it can only be judged in terms of its intention toward the visual medium. It exists somewhat like a set of notes for a translation: the finished translation can be judged as a work by itself, as can a film; but the notes for the translation can be judged only in terms of the intention toward the work. Noting this, Erwin Panofsky has pointed out that "the screenplay, in contrast to the theater play, *has no aesthetic existence independent of its performance, and . . . its characters have no aesthetic existence outside the actors.*" [7] Panofsky goes on:

The playwright writes in the fond hope that his work will be an imperishable jewel in the treasure house of civilization and will be presented in hundreds of performances that are but transient variations on a "work" that is constant. The script writer, on the other hand, writes for one producer, one director, and one cast. Their work achieves the same degree of permanence as does his; and should the same or a similar scenario ever be filmed by a different director and a different cast there will result an altogether different "play." [8]

The reasons for this are inherent in the medium itself: the cinema is much more complex than the stage, and a screenplay is much more flexible in the hands of a director than a stage play can ever be. Panofsky defines the specific possibilities of the cinema as *"dynamization of space* and, accordingly, *spatialization of time."* [9] In the theater "the spectator cannot leave his seat, and the setting of the stage cannot change, during one act," although "time, the medium of emotion and thought conveyable by speech, is free and independent of anything that may happen in visual space." [10] In the cinema, the situation is different:

Here, too, the spectator occupies a fixed seat, but only physically, not as the subject of an aesthetic experience. Aesthetically, he is in permanent motion as his eye identifies itself with the lens of the camera, which permanently shifts in distance and direction. And as movable as the spectator is, as movable is, for the same reason, the space presented to him. Not only bodies move in space, but space itself does, approaching, receding, turning, dissolving, and recrystallizing as it appears through the controlled locomotion and focusing of the camera and through the cutting and editing of the various shots—not to mention such special effects as visions, transformations, disappearances, slow-motion and fast-motion shots, reversals and trick films. This opens up a world of possibilities of which the stage can never dream.[11]

The result of all this, of course, is that the script, or whatever in the movie can be expressed with words, exists primarily as notes for the director, who is the true creator, since he works in the medium itself, whereas the scriptwriter does not. Thus, the artistic intention of the screenplay "differs in kind from that of a stage play, and much more from that of a novel or a piece of poetry." [12] The success of the movie script—"not unlike that of an opera libretto," [13] Panofsky adds—depends "not only upon its quality as a piece of literature, but also, or even more so, upon its integrability with the events on the screen." [14]

Agee's film treatments cover the whole range from

rough sketches, such as "Dedication Day," which is a strictly literary treatment of the material with no reference to the cinematic work, to *Noa Noa* with his extremely detailed notes on cutting, camera angles, sound qualities, and the expressions of the actors. With the exception of "Dedication Day," therefore, which can be discussed in purely literary terms, with some consideration of Agee's intention in calling it a rough sketch for "a moving picture," the scripts are very hard to criticize in terms of *any* medium; as Vernon Young pointed out in his review of *Agee on Film, Vol. II: Five Film Scripts*, "those filmed are already in a different category from the ones which haven't been; the latter invite either literary criticism under special conditions or speculations about works whose total realization has not taken place!"[15] The only way to criticize the scripts is, vaguely, as intentions.

In discussing, then, in the only terms that are possible, Agee's achievements as a scriptwriter, it may be well to make the distinction between adaptations and original work. The adaptations offer a possibility to examine Agee's notion of how a given material in one medium is to be translated into another medium, thereby suggesting the aesthetics that he is working with. The originals, conceived within the medium itself, show, with greater freedom, how Agee wanted to use the techniques of the visual medium to express certain ideas. The distinction between filmed and unfilmed scripts is, of course, irrelevant, if one assumes, as it is reasonable to do, the director as the "auteur"[16] or creator of the filmed work.

One problem of discussing adaptations is that commentators in general tend to judge the end result in one medium in terms of the original in another medium. Assuming that "content" is separable from "form," they tend to judge most deviations as a lack of respect for the original or as the result of cold-blooded commercialization. Failing to see that, as Mark Schorer says, technique "not only . . . *contains* intellectual and moral implications, but . . . *discovers* them," [17] they regard, much too often, the demands of the visual medium simply as decoration on a static material. The danger of this point of view should be self-evident, but even in a scholarly discussion of the subject, George Bluestone finds it necessary to warn against it:

What is common to all these assumptions is the lack of awareness that mutations are probable the moment one goes from a given set of fluid, but relatively homogeneous, conventions to another; that changes are *inevitable* the moment one abandons the linguistic for the visual medium. Finally, it is insufficiently recognized that the end products of novel and film represent different aesthetic genera, as different from each other as ballet is from architecture.[18]

For the adapter, thus, the work at hand is a matter of translating the material into a new language; Dudley Nichols, who adapted O'Flaherty's *The Informer* for John Ford's film version, suggests that this translation is a matter of finding a method "by which to make the psychological action photographic." [19] In this, the greatest responsibility in making changes is a result of the adapter's respect for the material: as Daniel Taradash (the scriptwriter for *From Here to Eternity*) has said, "You have to be bold in breaking away from the book when it becomes necessary." [20] Yet, finally, there are no definite rules for when this can or must be done, and when it cannot: the end result will be a testimony not primarily to the mere technique of the scriptwriter but, above all, to his good taste.

Agee's first published adaptation is a short treatment of

a part of André Malraux's novel *Man's Fate*, more specifically the section of Part Six where 200 Communists are waiting to be executed. What is immediately striking about Agee's notes is his clear documentary ambition. This is made abundantly clear in the notes which follow the treatment itself:

Important, on the fog, and on the timbre of film all the way through, to make this clear: that smooth and lyric fog (as in *Zoo in Budapest* or *The Informer*) is not meant and is to be avoided. By taking its resonance from that of the bell, I mean that that should be the rhythm of the grain in the film, as if produced of the sound. All the film should be grainy, hard black and white, flat focus, the stock and tone of film in war newsreels, etc., prior to the invention of panchromatic. No smoothness and never luminous. It should not seem to be fiction.

Much, here, could communicate in writing as postured, literary, and "artistic." In part, I think, because words slow it down. I don't know how in words to indicate that the cutting, for instance, would be dry and "dynamic" (vide *Arsenal*) rather than more heavily deliberated: or how to make clear that various head-groupings, faces, etc., would not be "composed" and romantic but literalness intensified to become formal out of its own substances. Much that through generalization here could easily seem slow and artistic could not be further particularized short of actual work in making the film. This particularization would all be directly opposed to this "fictional" or "lyric" suspicion.

The use of the disembodied voice and choric voices is of course exceedingly dangerous: they could with much difficulty avoid the mistakes made in the voicing of poetic radio plays. The problem would be to find the right voice—entirely untrained, un"cultivated" and above all unhistrionic; capable of coloring and intensifying a monotone without departing it.

The chorus voices, too: same desperate avoidance of the mass-chant type of tone: not in unison, very dry: voices not of poetic "performers" but of literal persons. When they sing the few notes its massiveness should come of many crowded and untrained voices, of which many sharpen and flat the pitch.[21]

This emphasis on the documentary technique, to the extent, even, of duplicating the grainy tone of war newsreels, is caused not only by Agee's particular preference but also by the actual theme of Malraux's novel. For *Man's Fate* is, as Haakon Chevalier points out in his introduction to it, both "a revolutionary document and . . . a work of art. The two are completely fused." [22] In showing fictive characters partaking in events that helped to shape history, the book opens the way for the kind of work which Agee was later to call "works of pure fiction, played against, and into, and in collaboration with unrehearsed and uninvented reality." [23] The immediacy of the screen image as well as its scientific correlation to the objects of the real world helps to annihilate the power of the suspension of disbelief which, finally, separates the work of art from reality itself.[24] The use of newsreel shots, a grainy film, and "un-'cultivated' " voices adds to this impression.

Although there is a fair amount of dialogue in Malraux, Agee does away with practically all of it, retaining only such commands and statements as are necessary for the action. Instead, he tries to visualize for the viewer the kind of human situation that exists in the prison. Compare, for instance, the two treatments of the episode of the Chinese who volunteers for his execution. Malraux writes:

Suddenly, one of the two unknown Chinese took a step forward, threw down his scarcely burnt cigarette, lit another after breaking two matches and went off with a hurried step towards the door, buttoning as he went, one by one, all the buttons of his coat. The door again shut.

One of the wounded was picking up the broken matches. His neighbors had broken into small fragments those from the box Lu Yu Hsuan had given them, and were playing at drawing straws.[25]

By adding to this a small detail and giving added emphasis to others, Agee manages to convey to the viewer the emotions of the Chinese as well as of those left behind and of the whole prison room in relationship to what is going on, all this without the use of words which, in the film, would merely slow down the perception of the reality:

. . . one of the men steps forward, the camera swinging with him; throws down his scarcely burnt cigaret (quick detail as it dryly hits the floor); walks two more steps and stops short. He has tried to turn his back and his face to everyone who might be watching him but the camera is watching him as, after breaking two matches, he lights another cigaret and draws in desperately deep on it and abruptly, the guard at his shoulder, resumes walking. Face tucked down, the cigaret stuck in it dragged on rapidly and smokily, buttoning carefully one by one all the buttons of his own coat, he walks quickly toward the camera (which is now at the door) and out the door, the camera swinging as he turns there and squaring into solid focus on the door which is immediately shut.

Immediate detail: the burning cigaret on the floor: a wounded man near it. The eyes of the two (Lu and his companion) looking at it, on the floor. The cigaret and the wounded man, who is thinking. After a little, with great delicateness and respect he reaches over his hand, takes the cigaret, and draws in on it, raising his eyes, as he lets out the smoke,

to Lu. Lu and his companion are watching him. They understand each other fully: (56)*

The point is that, although it is difficult to say whether
Agee's treatment is better or worse than Malraux's, by adding emphasis to certain details he manages to convey in
visually compact terms a situation that Malraux needed a
good many words and some dialogue for.

Similarly, Agee, in one place, uses a satiric montage to
expand the situation at hand. After cutting short the scream
of the prisoner being executed, he inserts three shots:

Swift shot (from newsreel) of Chiang Kai-shek at desk lifting
his face in a Methodist smile as if hearing a pleasant item of
conversation;
  of a woman in a night club, a questioning, listening look on
her face, asking an invisible companion to please repeat his
wisecrack;
  of a woman, in a small room in the city, who knows the
meaning of the whistle; and of her child, who does not . . .
(55)

While there is practically no dialogue in the film treatment, Agee prescribes an imaginative use of sound for
meaningful effect. During the first unbroken introductory
shot of the prison, we hear the whistle of the locomotive
into whose boiler the victims are thrown alive:

During this unbroken shot, which of course lasts less long
than it takes to describe, this is the sound: The whistle stays
on full blast. With the appearance of the three heads it is
added to itself: the same whistle in three other timbres.

With the next shot, as many dozens of timbres as possible:

* Page numbers in parentheses refer, in this discussion, to Agee,
"Man's Fate," *Films I* (November 1939), 51–60.

this shot is steep, from high, of the whole floor on which 200 men are prostrate. (52)

The effect suggested by this device is not only an impression that each man hears the whistle differently, but that there exists one whistle for each of them: they are all condemned to die.

The whistle is also used for other purposes. In the execution scene, we see a close-up of the face of the victim: "after not more than two seconds the face is exploded by the shriek and crazed over with intense steam. The shriek is that of the whistle" (55). This substitution is later reversed in the last shots of the treatment: the wire-puller's hand "jerks the wire down. Immediate human scream, intense and loud as possible" (59). Both these substitutions have great emotional shock value apart from their suggestions of the inhumanity and brutality of the situation. And after this high emotional pitch Agee suggests a release which also depends on sound:

. . . then with complete suddenness there is no steam, only the silent whistle that [sic], for four seconds, then deadblack screen: out of this screen a man's long, deep, emphatic sigh, of the utmost satisfaction of sex or gluttony, but also of the utmost remoteness, aloofness and solitude. Silence. Black screen. (60)

Kyo's meditation on the fate of the revolution, coming to the conclusion that "it is easy to die when one does not die alone," [26] is rendered by Malraux as an internal monologue. Agee first heightens our sense of the unreal here by showing us a few shots of Kyo's wife and father, indicating that this is Kyo's farewell, and then rendering the monologue, against a black screen, as a choric dialogue between Kyo and the other prisoners. This dialogue leads up to the moment when "the sorrowing of a multitude of men's voices increases and lifts and clarifies into rough-sung notes, in octaves and fifths, now joined with the voices of women, not loudly at all, but louder and brighter on each note" (59). This treatment of course, is hardly realistic or "documentary," but Agee is careful to maintain the level of unrehearsed reality by prescribing, in the notes already quoted, 'untrained, un'cultivated' and above all unhistrionic" voices (60). In the final chant, the "massiveness should come of many crowded and untrained voices, of which many sharpen and flat the pitch" (60). Thus, although the device as such is an element of fiction, its execution, due to the scientific accuracy of the recording apparatus, is kept on the level of objective realism.

It is worth noting here that when Agee reviewed Malraux's own film from the Spanish Civil War, *Man's Hope*, in 1947, he commented on many of the things that characterize his own treatment of *Man's Fate*. He found, for instance, the powerful combination of fiction and reality: the actors were "not merely amateurs but also fighters, in the last ditch of a lost war, whose 're-enactments' here were hardly that, pinched as they were into spare moments between actual work and actual war." [27] The movie seemed to go against all the "graces of art," but instead achieved "scrawny kinds of pace, immediacy, and personal detail which I have never before seen art attain." [28] Commenting on the scene where the dead and wounded are brought down from the mountain, Agee wrote:

I was so deeply moved by all I saw, and by Malraux's confidence in the grandeur of the interlocked fact and symbol, and by his determination to build this wonderful symbol through a virtually endless series of near-repetitions into a colossal dirge for heroes, that for me it towered above most successes, and most attempts, that I have ever seen in films.[29]

It is this "confidence in the grandeur of the interlocked fact and symbol" which is at the heart of Agee's aesthetics, both as a critic and as a scriptwriter, and it characterizes his treatment of *Man's Fate* more eloquently than any other script of his.

Agee's adaptation of Stephen Crane's short story "The Blue Hotel" was his first commercial script, and as such it lacks the deeply passionate involvement of his treatment of *Man's Fate*. Shots are simply characterized as close, medium, or long, in the standard manner, and there is little of the intricate compositions that occur in the earlier work.

On the whole, Agee follows Crane closely. He finds the basic meaning of the story in the Easterner's final speech:

Every sin is the result of a collaboration. We, five of us, have collaborated in the murder of this Swede. Usually there are from a dozen to forty women really involved in every murder, but in this case it seems to be only five men—you, I, Johnnie, old Scully; and that fool of an unfortunate gambler came merely as a culmination, the apex of a human movement, and gets all the punishment.[30]

In the script, this statement becomes simplified: "Every sin is a collaboration. Everybody is responsible for everything," [31] but the basic meaning is still there, and the structure of the script strives to emphasize exactly what Crane calls "a culmination, the apex of a human movement." To this end, Agee transposes some of the material in order to give the film a dramatic continuity that was not necessary for Crane. In the short story, for instance, the last episode, with the Easterner's confession of guilt and his statement that Johnnie did really cheat, comes several months after the events themselves, and, furthermore, involves only the Easterner, who has been serving as the reasonable focus of the story, and the cowboy who, "injured and rebellious," [32] refuses to accept any responsibility whatsoever; Scully and Johnnie are left entirely out of it. Agee places the Easterner's accusation against Johnnie immediately after the Swede has left the hotel but before he has been killed; and he uses the symbolism implicit in Crane's title ("The Palace Hotel at Fort Romper was painted a light blue, a shade that is on the legs of a kind of heron, causing the bird to declare its position against any background" [33]) to emphasize the responsibility of all of them in case anything should happen to the Swede:

Good heavens, we flatter ourselves we're civilized men . . . fit to cope with Destiny, Fate, the Devil Himself. And we come up against some puzzling minor disturbance like this Swede, and all we can do is the worst that's in us. (a strange, almost clairvoyant bitterness) Oh, *we declared ourselves,* all right . . . as sure as that blue-legged heron! Yes, indeed! *We* made him what he's become tonight. *We're* the ones who've put him in danger!   (469)*

The Easterner leaves the hotel, and the others follow him, but when they arrive at the bar, they find the Swede already dead. Scully is concerned only that his and Johnnie's involvement in the Swede's death not be made public in town; but the Easterner has his conscience to live with:

With the absolute silence an even more fierce and living quiet intensifies in the Easterner's face and becomes, as well, sorrow,

* Page numbers in parentheses, in the following discussion, refer to *Agee on Film, Col II; Five Film Scripts* (New York: McDowell, Obolensky, 1960)

pity, tenderness, a passionate desire for, and hopelessness of, expiation. The face rises on a high wave of realization, almost transfigured, on the verge, even, of mysticism, yet iron, virile, tragic—as, very slowly, his eyes still fixed toward the Swede, he walks into extreme CLOSE UP and PAST THE CAMERA out of the shot. (487–488)

And Agee adds a final image to emphasize the universal involvement in the guilt of one man: (". . . the cold stars sharpen; and very slowly, like a prodigious wheel, the whole sky begins to turn." [34])

The total effect of these changes is to shift the emphasis from Crane's realization of the irony of the "apex of a human movement" which will hit an "innocent" man to a more tragic realization that every man must live with his guilt of collaboration in all sins. This shift can be defended (if this is necessary at all) on the grounds that it is already implicit in Crane's story, and that Crane's irony, which depends mostly on the swift *verbal* revelation at the conclusion, would have been virtually impossible to render satisfactorily in *visual* terms without violating the rest of the story.

Apart from this shift of emphasis, most of Agee's changes in or additions to the original story are simply matters of expanding the characterizations. The Swede, in particular, receives a much fuller treatment in Agee's script. When he offers to leave the hotel, for instance, he is made to realize, in Agee's version, that "the apex of a human movement" will be reached no matter what:

SWEDE. Never mind, Mr. Scully; never mind. I know *you* don't want trouble, but *you* can't stop them. *N*obody can stop them, not God Himself. (sad wag of head) No Mr. Scully, I will go away. I do not wish to be killed. (418)

And a short while later, when Scully comes to his room, the Swede says: "Just one rule, Mr. Scully, and I learned it young. Don't never trust *no*body. Be ready for *any*thing" (420). The Swede's behavior during six o'clock supper, which Crane sums up in one paragraph, is given almost five pages in Agee's treatment, which not only emphasizes the Swede's over-confidence but also shows how superficial it is by inserting a scene in which the Swede is frightened by the noise of the wind in the chimney.

Agee follows Crane closely enough to be able to use and, to some extent, even expand his symbols. In the beginning of the story, Crane mentions the view from the front-room window: "A gatepost like a still man with a blanched face stood aghast amid this profligate fury." [35] Agee uses this image three times; the first time it appears, there is no explicit connection with the story: "CLOSE SHOT—THROUGH THE FRONT WINDOW OF THE MAIN ROOM. Extreme violence of snow and wind, the only visual anchorage is a blanched gatepost leaning rigid into it" (405). The second time, its connection with the Swede is made clear: he is looking out the window and "CAMERA SLOWLY TURNS square on the window to focus on what his eyes are fixed on —the post" (408). Finally, the image of the Swede just as he has knocked out Johnnie for the last time associates back to the gatepost:

MEDIUM SHOT—THE SWEDE—FROM EASTERNER'S ANGLE. He is leaning heavily against a little wind-waved tree, breathing like an engine, while his savage and flame-lit eyes roam from face to face . . . a mysterious and lonely figure, waiting . . . a splendor of isolation in his situation. (452)

There are few daring strokes of pure cinematic technique in Agee's script. In a few places he suggests using the sound track imaginatively: the scene at the dinner table, frightening the Swede; and when all of them go out for the fight, Agee wants a special sound effect to emphasize the almost supernatural violence of the storm:

FULL SOUND of a very strong wind, but more compelling than any other noise, a pure electric or electronic sound, without timbre, either so high it is just at the limit of audibility or so high that it is just beyond that limit and works purely on the nervous system (experiment will determine which is better used in this context). (445)

The camera technique is, on the whole, rather conventionally outlined. On only two occasions does Agee suggest shots of more than passing interest. The first occurs when the Swede has just accused Johnnie of cheating:

CAMERA, starting with a shot past the Swede's head, centering on Johnnie MEDIUM CLOSE, makes, fairly fast and accelerating, steadily tighter and faster and closer, the circling movement by which a tethered heifer winds herself up short around a post. The players meanwhile are all simultaneously repeating their lines as heretofore with only very close ad lib variations . . . As the CAMERA thus ropes them in they all close tighter and tighter against one center as if it were literally a rope around them: they come as close as five people can get. The ROUNDING CAMERA, at shoulder height, SWINGS through an extreme CLOSE UP of the Swede past Johnnie's head and then of Johnnie past the Swede's head practically as if they were waltzing, and comes to a stop, very close in, profiling Johnnie's glaring head at l.s. [left stage] and the Swede's in r.s. [right stage]. (440)

The second is the shot of the Swede working his way from the hotel to the town:

It is to be heightened above realism, during the Swede's advance up the boardwalk. When he is still in the deepest distance, we use only every third frame; then every second; then cut every third frame; then every fourth; meanwhile slurring the CAMERA speed a little, fewer frames per second, so that his speed of approach is at all times superhuman and grotesque, but becomes smoother as he approaches. By the time his features become distinct no frames are skipped but the motion, though regular, is fast and dry rather than silky . . . As he comes into full close up, shade back to normal speed, omitting no frames. The SOUND runs smooth, not clipped; it is not recorded on the spot. (464)

Both these shots would have their own particular effectiveness in context, one imagines, and Agee's descriptions show that he was aware of the possibility of heightening certain effects through purely technical means: the first shot, in fact, would symbolize the general movement of the characters in the story: how their involvement leads to a point where an explosion becomes necessary; and the second shot would present the Swede's own conception of himself after the fight.

On the whole, however, the script is not remarkably original. For one thing, it would seem that in any commercial movie project the scriptwriter must realize that it is finally the director who decides how the shots are to be filmed, and it is the duty of the writer to provide an outline, the basic *mise-en-scene*. Essentially, this explains the difference between the scripts that Agee wrote for himself, such as "Man's Fate," and those that he wrote under contract, such as "The Blue Hotel."

Finally, although most of Agee's prose is here utilitarian, as it must be in a script, it has a tendency to be excessively descriptive; and it may be asked if even the actors could use some of Agee's suggestions. In one scene, the Easterner is supposed to be "looking even smaller than he is" (429); in the final scene, already quoted, the actor of that role would have to express, with his face, a "fierce and living quiet" as well as "sorrow, pity, tenderness, a passionate desire for, and hopelessness of, expiation" (487-488). This is a tall order, and although the description may be of some use to the director and the actor, it is the result here of a basically literary, rather than cinematic, imagination. In another place, Agee suggests that the proper way to pronounce a certain "squeezed curse" is to "try saying the first 2/3ds of 'God' and 'Christ' simultaneously, from between tight teeth" (448), and that the Swede's "wild animal snarl" is "roughly, *Arghrgh*" (450); the usefulness of both suggestions may be questioned. Still, this close conception of details indicates an awareness of the totality of the work, which, although it may be impractical, is certainly honorable in its artistic intention.

The African Queen, which Agee wrote in 1950, is, as Dwight Macdonald puts it, "mostly just another movie, but it does have several Agee touches." [36] Agee himself made a just observation on it in a letter to Father Flye while the work was still in progress:

If everything works out right, it could be a wonderful movie. If much works out wrong, it can be lousier than most. I think most likely it will wind up as good, maybe even very good, but not wonderful, or lousy. The work is a great deal of fun: treating it fundamentally as high comedy with deeply ribald undertones, and trying to blend extraordinary things—poetry, mysticism, realism, romance, tragedy, with the comedy . . .[37]

Not all of this comes through in the script itself (or, for that matter, in the finished film). Basically, the subject is treated as high comedy, making, above all, a distinction between decorum and the kind of success that counts (such as sailing a boat down the rapids); this distinction extends to include that between Rose and Allnutt, or that between the mission and the river, or, finally, that between the Germans and the English. It is made hilariously clear in a scene which is of Agee's invention: Allnutt having tea with Rose and her brother:

INT. DINING ROOM. MED. SHOT—RIGIDLY SYMMETRICAL, ACROSS DINING ROOM TABLE:
Rose at dead center, Brother at her left, in profile, Allnutt at her right, opposite Brother, in profile. The room is so shaded against heat it is gloomy. The silence, gloom and heat are stifling. Rose is pouring the second of three cups of tea; she pours the third. Brother is deep in the news of a Mission paper. Allnutt sits oppressed by the silence, like a child on his good behavior. A long silence while Rose leisurely pours. (156)

In this atmosphere of oppressively middle-class decorum, emphasized by the rigidly symmetrical camera, Allnutt's stomach begins to growl:

All of a sudden, out of the silence, there is a SOUND like a mandolin string being plucked. At first the sound is unidentifiable, though instantly all three glance sharply up, each at the other two, then away; in the next instant they recognize what it is and each glances sharply, incredulously, at the other two —and then again, quickly away: then Brother and Rose glance with full recognition at Allnutt, at the instant that he knows the bellygrowl is his. At the moment of recognition, he glances down at his middle with a look of embarrassed reproach. He glances up quickly and slyly—hopeful they've missed it—to find the eyes of both still fixed on him. The instant their eyes meet they bounce apart like billiard balls, and fix on the first neutral object they happen to hit. Then Allnutt looks at them again: neither will look at him. (157)

The scene goes on, but this is enough to show that, coming as it does in the beginning of the film, it focuses the attention on the break of decorum, which is the theme of the film (as well as the source for the comedy): Rose, the sister of a missionary, falling in love with Allnutt, a dirty Cockney skipper, or *The African Queen*, a decrepit old launch, sinking *The Louisa*, a hundred-ton steamer.

As always, Agee pays close attention to details: the picture of the fainted missionary is a remarkable blend of fiction and uncomfortable reality:

He is piteous, absurd, and ugly; sprawled out on the floor as ill-shaped as a wounded bat, with his nightshirt partly on, shrouding his head, and his trousers half off, trammeling knees which are grotesquely angled. Between lowered pants and hiked-up nightshirt, a sad, humiliating expanse of long white drawers in this furnace weather. His feet are fouled-up in his suspenders. The SHOT is to be both preposterous and shocking. (166)

Occasionally, this attention to details again leads to excessively descriptive directions to the actors, as when Rose "looks as if she had cried herself dry, and she looks as if she might quite possibly be dead" (241), or when "her face becomes quietly transcendent" (243). Likewise, the following shot is something less than visual:

MEDIUM SHOT—THE BOILER AND ENGINE HEAD-
ON like an altar. Allnutt lounges in one side of the SHOT
like an acolyte, and quietly watches toward Rose, steering.
(185))

All in all, however, the impression remains that this is
a competent but not extraordinary script, and this is
ironically underscored by the fact that Agee's work on
The African Queen was nominated for an Academy
Award. In fact, that impression holds true of most of his
commercial scripts. His second adaptation of a Stephen
Crane story, *The Bride Comes to Yellow Sky*, written in
1951–52 and released together with another short picture
under the title *Face to Face*, is equally competent and,
one might almost add, equally uninteresting. There are,
however, nice touches which suggest Agee at his best.

The theme of Crane's story, as Agee sees it, is the conflict of codes and behavior. The old code of the West is
breaking down in Yellow Sky: the marshal goes to San
Antonio to find a wife, and Scratchy Wilson, the last
outlaw around, wears, in Crane's words, "a maroon-
colored flannel shirt, which had been purchased for purposes of decoration, and made principally by some Jewish
women on the East Side of New York" [38] and boots "of
the kind beloved in winter by little sledding boys on the
hillsides of New England." [39] To stress this situation right
at the beginning of the movie, Agee shows the marshal
leaving town and telling a prisoner to be sure to lock himself in after he has had his meals at the saloon: hardly
the stereotyped Western situation. Later, when Scratchy
Wilson is prowling through town, Agee adds a scene
where he attacks, verbally as well as actively, the bour-

geois respectability of Jasper Morgan and Deacon Smeed, two upstanding citizens of the town. To add even further to the illusion of the breakdown of the Western code, Agee has the prisoner (who is an addition to the story) say that he is tired of reading "all that bang-bang stuff" (368) in the magazines in jail. And when the marshal carries his bride over the threshold of their home, the prisoner drops from his cell (which is situated above the home) confetti made of "the torn pictures of the murderous faces and weapons of early western fiction" (390).

Thus, if Agee's adaptation of Crane's story is primarily a skillful translation of certain material from one medium to another, it also exhibits his unerring sense of the meaningful elements of Crane's original. Sometimes, this is even expressed in cinematic technique, as when Agee makes a transition from Scratchy Wilson's "real shocker of a necktie," dragged "drunkenly, snakily, slithering from its hook," to "Potter's more conservative tie," which he adjusts, "tense and uneasy" (372). On the principle that a transition connects two symbolically important details, this extreme focus on two ties seems somewhat comical (for added emphasis Agee here uses the iris out-iris in device).

It should also be recognized that the limitations of Agee's script are, to a certain extent, the limitations of Crane's original. For, as a comedy of manners, Crane's story depends on the conflict between the rough code of the West and the polite manners of the East, and although the tragedy of the failure to adapt from one code to the other is presented in comic terms, the West has become so firmly entrenched in the American legends that it is hard to perceive the universality of the conflict: the comic aspects are more dominant than the larger, tragic ones.

The last of Agee's adaptations, *The Night of the*

Hunter, which was made into a movie under the direction of Charles Laughton, is just as skillful as his other adaptations. Agee treats Davis Grubb's novel as straight melodrama with some memorable devices, as the opening helicopter shot of children playing along the river, to the accompaniment of the Biblical quote about false prophets in sheep's clothing. Otherwise, the most interesting thing about the script is that it is so different from Laughton's finished product. As Andrew Sarris has pointed out, the final shooting script is rumored to be "one-third Laughton, one-third James Agee and one-third Davis Grubb"; and the film "displays a striking visual style, almost semi-Germanic Griffith, which is completely lacking in the Huston-Agee-Forester *The African Queen* and the Windust-Agee-Crane *The Bride Comes to Yellow Sky*." [40] This style is, for that matter, completely lacking even in Agee's script on Grubb's novel. Also, it is somewhat surprising that Agee, with his extensive knowledge of the South and the Depression, did not try to put more of that experience into the script.

Agee's three original film scripts or scenarios are all rather more interesting than his adaptations because they give him a freer rein to work out his own relationship with the medium. "The House," published in 1937, is a poetic-satiric allegory which works mainly through a radical montage of images. Consider, for instance, the parade which occurs early in the outline:

From far down the length of street opens martial band music, tremendously loud and tremendously distant. A few bars of this (the music continues and gets louder throughout the following until at the end it is as nearly deafening as possible) and almost at the horizon of the street pale forms, in a block, down the middle of the street, transparent and frail as locust shells, can be seen marching: they are very diminutive, far out of scale with the street and the buildings. There is a loud noise of dry blown leaves while they are still pale, which, as they materialize, materializes into the sound of distant marching. As they advance and solidify in time to the (invisible) band, they are seen to be not more than two or three troops of uniformed Boy Scouts (with one or two tall leaders) surrounding a float upon which stands a crucifix. For as long as three minutes the camera is absolutely stationary: then, first with flickerlike flashes and later with a more jabbing and steady rhythm, the basic position-one shot is crosslanced (not in double exposure) with swift intimate detail of childish feet grinding faces of Negroes, Jews; a heel twisting out the lenses of horn-rimmed spectacles; a little hand grabbing at an open book and ripping out leaves (blood springs after); hands (childish) belaboring drums, cymbals, hornkeys, gripping brass knuckles, blackjacks; hefting the butts of rifles; closeup, from low, of the advanced, pure, sadistic jaw-head of a scoutmaster; of a second scoutmaster; of a swastikaed armband. In none of these shots are faces shown. As they advance it becomes clear that the crucifix is not a crucifix but a stripped woman, handless and footless, nailed by her wrists and shins to the cross, whose lowered head with its tresses of drenched weeping willow is a schoolboy globe of the earth. The sign tacked above her reads, in crayoned school letters, MOTHER. It further becomes clear that the Boy Scouts are not boys but adult midgets, and their faces, now ranked advancing in the camera, are military, bloodthirsty and aloof in the midget way. Once this midget fact has been opened there are swift shots also of a midget financier, a midget war orator, midget mothers and sweethearts leaning from windows, waving flags, scattering confetti and paper flowers, and, through the now utmost loudness of brass music, cheering in midget voices.[41]

In itself, this passage is not as original as it may seem: similar experiments with montage and free association were carried on rather extensively in the thirties by such *avant-garde* filmmakers as Jean Cocteau *(Le Sang d'un Poete)*, Salvador Dali *(Le Chien Andalou)*, and Luis Buñuel *(L'Age d'Or)*. What *is* remarkable in Agee's outline is the extreme sharpness of the images and the clear sense of the satiric purpose which binds them together. With only a few juxtaposed images, Agee manages to suggest that the militant aspects of the Boy Scouts, under the guise of Christianity (which is made to reveal itself, in this context, as a cruel abuse of womanhood in the name of respect for motherhood) are equivalent to the sadistic attitude of the Nazis toward Negroes, Jews, and all scholarly learning in the world, and that this "military, bloodthirsty" development is as shrunkenly inhuman as a midget seems to be in relationship to a normal man. Furthermore, appearing as it does in "a middle-sized provincial industrial city (one hundred thousand to two hundred thousand population; say Knoxville or Chattanooga, Tenn.),"[42] the parade is not just a parade but an image of the political climate in America in the mid-thirties.

The political nature of the story is evident throughout. The owners of a Victorian house, described with the most outrageous symbols, leave in a black limousine; the servants pocket the silverware and leave; when time has run out (symbolized by a speeded-up clock whose hands fall off), the house is destroyed by water, and the old woman who still occupies it is drowned. Later, poor children playing in the gutter find remnants of the house and its occupants: a little girl makes a bridal veil out of a lace curtain; another child a toga out of a black skirt. With great solemnity, they bury a dead goldfish (which has previously been seen in the house).

This story is told without dialogue (but with sound)

in heavily symbolic pictures. The owners of the house, for instance, all have their symbolic attributes: the old man has "his face made up chalk white, his eyebrows very black" and is costumed for "a political funeral"; another man, appearing in the upper half of executive and the lower half of golfing costume, "carries a mashie with formal fragility, like something between a scepter and a lily"; a woman dressed in a girdle and a nearly transparent dress carries next to her heart "a discolored and exhausted phallus from whose glans, pulling a long hole in the flesh, droops a wide wedding ring"; a young man, "wearing a checked sports coat and otherwise a tuxedo," carries "a cocktail glass brimful of lightly fuming acid, and of this he must not spill a drop"; a beautiful young woman has her skull "closed in a pessary" and carries "a clear globe in whose center, sustained in alcohol, hangs a miniature foetus in a baby bonnet"; and "an over-developed girl of nine" has a "submergedly desperate nympholeptic face." [43]

Seen with the hindsight of twenty-five years, this kind of surrealistic symbolism seems rather heavy-handed, and for all its effectiveness in its particular context, one is tempted to quote what Agee wrote ten years later about Vittorio de Sica's *Shoeshine:*

Almost every minute of it has a kind of rashness, magnanimity, and deep, wise emotional directness which, I am convinced, can hardly if at all exist in a piece of work unless those who make it are sure they are at one with a large, eager, realistic general audience . . .[44]

For that kind of "emotional directness" "The House" is far too ambitious. Nevertheless, the script shows Agee's awareness of the possibilities to use the film camera for a symbolic poetry which is rarely seen on the screen. His descriptions of isolated shots are extremely precise and often suggest the emotional quality to be gained:

This general garden shot has been very slightly out of focus: not fuzzy and not sentimental, but enough out of focus to generalize it and to put a white dusty summer brightness upon everything in sight. With the last few inches of largo panning the focus quite as slowly cleanses and comes to maximum sharpness and black-and-whiteness: whole quality of emotion should be that of a microscope slide drawn into razor focus and from now on totally at the mercy of the lens.[45]

"Dedication Day," which was published in 1946, is subtitled a "rough sketch for a moving picture."[46] There is little, however, to suggest why Agee thought this material would make a suitable movie: the scenario is written in a straightforward literary manner,[47] with no directions for camera work and other cinematic details.

This, too, is a satire which attacks the official attitude that would build a monument to the atomic bomb and consider any efforts at atonement proof of insanity. Within the framework of this basic reversal, Agee manages to attack practically all facets of "official" culture and taste: Frank Lloyd Wright, Louis Aragon, Harry Brown, Robert E. Sherwood, the Catholic Church, the Protestant Church, the Jewish faith, Herbert H. Lehman, the Eagle Scouts, Morton Gould, James Bryan Conant, the President, Charles de Gaulle, the Chinese Purchasing Commission, Rehabilitation Loans, Norman Bel Geddes, the food in the armed services, the Gallup polls, psychoanalysts, philosophers, and clergymen in general. The persona or mask that Agee adopts for this attack is not immediately identifiable, for with the exception of a few sententious remarks ("Such are the unfortunate effects of a single man's unbridled individualism"–261),* the writing is largely objective: one could imagine the writer as a conscentious reporter for a semi-sophisticated monthly journal. But the satire is not in the writing; it is in the basic conception of the situation itself. Thus, everything in the story relates back to the stupidity and ignorance which fail to see the atomic bomb as a crime which demands sacrifice and atonement, but builds a monument to "memorialize the greatest of human achievements" (252). When Agee seems to criticize Frank Lloyd Wright, it is even more the official attitude behind him that is the target:

The Arch, which had been designed by Frank Lloyd Wright, was the master-builder's sole concession to the Romanesque; at that, he had made it proof against frost, earthquakes, and the inscription and carving of initials. (252)

Here, Wright is a symbol for the pretentiousness of official taste and the utilitarian tendency in American life to "proof" material objects against natural processes. Likewise, when Agee writes that the Japanese who work inside the monument to produce the Eternal Fuse burning above ground are required to eat what American soldiers eat, his list of that food becomes a parody of the official concept of what is "American":

. . . one can of K Rations, two four-pound porterhouse steaks, one carton of Camels, eight squares of Ex-Lax, two boxes of Puffed Rice, the juice of twelve oranges, a tin of Spam, a cup of Ovaltine, a prophylactic, a tube of nationally

* Page numbers in parentheses refer, in this discussion, to "Dedication Day," as reprinted in *New Directions 10* (New Jersey: New Directions, 1948) pp. 252–63.

advertised toothpaste, and macerated or liquified overseas editions of *Time, Reader's Digest* and the New Testament, each, per day, plus roast beef, apple pie and store cheese on Sundays and proper supplements, including third helpings, spoonlickings and ejaculations of "Gosh, Mom," of the special dishes traditionally appropriate to the major Holidays; all to be administered orally, rectally or by intravenous injection, as best befitted the comfort of the individual patient—a task which many of the little fellows found so embarrassing, and which the tourists found so rightly amusing to watch, that even after the first few days, feeding time created something of a traffic problem. (256)

The hilarity and sure sense of exaggeration in this passage reveals, in fact, deep anger and fierce resentment toward those who use their appreciation of all good things American to look down on others.

Agee also satirizes a society which nominally gives full scope to all religions, yet refuses to recognize the significance of such concepts as "atonement," "guilt," "individual responsibility," and "sacrifice." The visitors observing the atomic scientist who volunteered to work on the Eternal Fuse with the Japanese note "that as he worked he spoke, and that his speech was evidently a terrible blended stream of self-vilification and of pr–y–r" (260). After the scientist has committed suicide, as "a kind of religious or ethical 'sacrifice'" (262), psychoanalysts and philosophers start studying his case, and clergymen use the incident as a lesson for such "as find themselves for any reason of pride, or a thirst for undue publicity, liable to the grievous error of exaggerated scrupulousness" (263); their text, of course, is "Render unto Caesar the things that are Caesar's, and unto God the things that are God's." And in a final twist to the satire, the reporter of the events grants that maybe there was a sort of "sacrifice" in the scientist's action:

For misguided and altogether regrettable though his last days were—a sad warning indeed to those who turn aside from the dictates of reason, and accept human progress reluctantly —he was nevertheless, perhaps, our last link with a not-too-distant past in which such conceptions as those of "atonement," and "guilt," and "individual responsibility," still had significance. And, in a sense, his gift to mankind was greater, perhaps, than that of his more stable colleagues. For, though "sacrifice" is a word to be used only with apologies, it would be hard to define what, if anything, they "sacrificed" in the giving; but he gave up his sanity. (263)

The effectiveness of satire depends on the verisimilitude of either the persona of the writer or the events themselves. As stated earlier, Agee depends more on the events than on the speaker's attitude; and one of the impressive things about "Dedication Day" is that, for all the exaggerations and sometimes outrageous suggestions, the whole seems at first absolutely convincing. The loudspeakers concealed within the monument, the special performance of Beethoven's Ninth Symphony, the closed-circuit television, the blessings of Cardinals, "their voices blended with that of the Pontifical Benediction, relayed from Rome" (253), the Protestant clergymen, "each, between his closed eyes, pinching the bridge of his nose between thumb and forefinger as if adjusting an invisible pair of pince-nez" (254), the "exquisite little girl," her "bladder a trifle unstabilized by privilege" (254), and the speeches, "more notable for resonance, eloquence, and on every speaker's part a most scrupulous courtesy and optimism, than for understanding, far less communication of understanding"

(253), all this is so close to truth that one could easily be deceived. Wyndham Lewis was, in fact, deceived, at first; he wrote in a letter to Dwight Macdonald:

A thing of Agee's [sic] was terribly good I thought—about the incontinence of a sweet little girl, at the climax of a solemn ceremony of dedication. (I thought at first it was something that had really happened: it was the dear little girl that opened my eyes to the deception.) [48]

There is no indication in the story itself as to why Agee thought it would be suitable for a motion picture. Clearly, however, the fact that the satire is in the events themselves, rather than in the speaker's voice, makes the story suitable for a satiric movie in the manner of newsreels or documentaries, and the few instances when the persona carries the satire could be presented as part of a stereotyped TV or film commentary.[49]

Agee's last script, *Noa Noa*, was never filmed. Apart from his use of biographies, Agee follows Gauguin's own journal very closely, at times word by word. One can understand why he would be fascinated by the subject matter: throughout the script one finds themes that relate to all of the basic notions in Agee's own work. Agee once suggested that he trusted "only the individualist in art," [50] and in the script Gauguin's answer, when Bertin asks him who does the world's work and who holds civilization together, expresses this kind of individualism:

Gauguin's reactions to "world's work" and "civilization" are quiet, but ferociously contemptuous.
GAUGUIN (calm; smiling) The cowards. The fools. The rabbits. Those who have no talent to betray, and those who lack the courage to be true to it.[51]

Gauguin also expresses a basic notion of Agee's that reality is beautiful but the artificial not, when he says: "The ugly can be beautiful, Madam; the pretty, never." [52] Gauguin's search for "the lost innocence of the human race . . . a place in this world where human beings live like all the other plants and the animals under the sun" [53] echoes Agee's conviction that the tenant farmers in the South lived a life much more real than his own "sophisticated" existence as journalist and spy.[54] Finally, Gauguin's life, which seems, at first, a total failure, but is turned into a victory by his ability to endure, as Agee has Vernier say, "great suffering, with great courage, for a great purpose," [55] exemplifies Agee's conviction that a failure which is totally true to its own determining factors is, paradoxically, a "success": in its truth to itself it has more meaning than a shallow and insincere success.

This view of Gaughin's life is evident even in the structure of the script. Agee makes it a flashback, beginning with Gaughin's death, at a point when nearly everyone condemns him; but when we reach the conclusion, that failure has become a victory and his death something which brought forth fruit (illustrating the motto Agee used for the film, "Except a grain of wheat fall into the ground and die, it abideth alone: but if it die, it bringeth forth much fruit," from St. John). This basic movement of the film is made clear on other levels as well: in the beginning of the script, Gauguin objects to Van Gogh's hysteric religiosity, although he can see in Vincent himself an image of the suffering Christ: "all the while I was painting that portrait, what I saw, was Christ on the Cross"; [56] but when Gauguin has died, Agee's imagery suggests a sensual rather than suffering and sentimental Christ:

As we TILT DOWNWARD he reverently places upon the raw earth a huge blood-red flower. As soon as he does, a bee dives into it like a bullet (most easily gotten by reversing a shot??) and we begin to understand the strange o.s. [off stage] humming. Tioka, beginning to understand it, glances to one side and up as we PAN in, close over Gauguin's own, new, nameless, wooden cross, to the foot of a great Crucifix and the snow-white, weather-split feet of a wooden Corpus. Tioka, turning, comes again into the shot, looking: there are a few bees, and the split feet, from inside, sweat and seep out a rich, golden honey. After looking for a moment, Tioka, with sad and elderly childlike curiosity, tips one finger into the honey; licks it; looks up to the face of the Christ o.s.; and walks out of the shot.

Now if we have a crane we RISE STRAIGHT UP the entire bee-dwelt, honey-swollen body of Christ, culminating with the head. Otherwise,

CUT TO CLOSE SHOT—HEAD OF THE CHRIST

Split and weathered, crowned with thorns, very beautiful, profoundly victorious in utter defeat, the dying Head is fallen to the left, and the dying Eyes gaze out over the Valley of Atuona (o.s.). There are bees here, too, on the face and on the eyes and among the thorns; the sound of their humming is immortally strong; and here, too, the rich gold of the wild honey seeps through.[57]

The director Joseph Mankiewicz has suggested that *Noa Noa* is such a complete blueprint for a motion picture that a "director could shoot it without ever saying an original word." [58] Although this is not necessarily a virtue in a film script (the nature of which is to be a draft for work in another medium), there are, in *Noa Noa*, passages which are impressive as proof of Agee's cinematic imagination. The sequence with Christ on the Cross is one of them; another one is the sequence about Gauguin's first "true" erotic meeting with Tehura, which, using "ultra-sensuous detail shots, almost orgiastically rich in form and color, of flowers, foliage, fruit, portions of faces and bodies of men, women and children" as well as shots "of the most voluptuous of Gauguin's paintings of that period," [59] succeeds in linking fiction and reality to the advantage of both.

Two other sequences are remarkable for the extremely close detail with which Agee works out the cutting. One is the king's funeral, which, according to Agee's directions, "is to be cut rigidly to the music of Chopin's Funeral March"; [60] he proceeds to outline the shots, sometimes as many as eight, for each beat. As if this were not enough, he also suggests that "the scoring, and performance, should be those of a French deep provincial military band of the period: rather shrill and squeaky, and not very well played; yet with genuine solemnity." [61] The other sequence is Gauguin's fishing expedition with the natives, which is cut rhythmically in time to the stroking of the canoes.[62] It is impossible to suggest anything definite about these sequences without seeing them filmed; as they stand, however, they testify to Agee's ambition to employ the medium for its own visual, rather than literary, effects.

Summing up Agee's career as a scriptwriter, one must concede that it is less spectacular than is generally suggested. Many of his scripts seem, in cinematic terms, conventional and unoriginal. On the other hand, it should be pointed out, first of all, that they are considerably freer from clichés than most commercial products: one is afraid to think of what a standard Hollywood adaptation might have made of "The Bride Comes to Yellow Sky" or "The

Blue Hotel." Secondly, to complain, as Vernon Young has done, that Agee's scripts are not visual enough,[63] is to judge the scripts according to the standards of a medium to which they do not belong: the most that Agee's scripts can do is tell us his awareness of cinema as well as demonstrate his use of his own interests and themes in that particular medium. They cannot tell us of his stature as film artist because he simply did not touch the medium himself.

Thus, the importance of Agee's scripts in the evaluation of his total career is not that they are good and bad but that they show us his enduring faith in the truth and beauty of the "real" world, ugly or not, his sense of the significance of the detail, accepted on its own terms, and his passionate involvement in the glory and tragedy of the human individual, as well as his hopes for a new poetry in the cinema, of "pure fiction, played against, and into, and in collaboration with unrehearsed and uninvented reality." [64]

V

LITERATURE AS
TRANSFIGURED REALITY

FICTION

During the last five years of his life, Agee did not work
exclusively with films: he also produced three prose works
of consistently high quality. The first of these was a
novella about the experiences of a young boy during the
night between Maundy Thursday and Good Friday, *The
Morning Watch*. The first draft of this was finished in
May 1950; [1] it was published first in *Partisan Review*, in
March 1951, [2] and a month later issued in book form by
Houghton Mifflin. The following year, his short story "A
Mother's Tale" appeared in *Harper's Bazaar*. [3] Finally,
Agee worked for a good many years on *A Death in the
Family* without ever finishing it properly; it was published
posthumously in 1957 and received the Pulitzer Prize in
1958. In a letter to Father Flye in 1948, Agee mentions
it as "a novel, short but longer than I had foreseen or
thought best for it, about my first 6 years, ending the
day of my father's burial." [4] The final version, of course,
centers almost exclusively on the death and burial of his

father, except for the italicized sections which the editors have placed in the beginning and immediately after Parts I and II.

Since *The Morning Watch* and *A Death in the Family* are closely related in style as well as in the autobiographical nature of the experience, it seems convenient to treat them together. The following discussion of Agee's fiction will, therefore, begin with "A Mother's Tale."

I

The plot is simple and eloquent. A young calf, seeing a huge herd of cattle being driven eastward, asks his mother for an explanation. The mother tells him the story of The One Who Came Back: how the cattle are driven out on the range, how they are put in a train and travel far, how they are finally unloaded and led into a strange house with a strange smell where, one by one, they meet The Man With The Hammer who brings his instrument down on their foreheads as they pass beneath him. The young calf is not convinced by his mother's story; he still wants to go out on the range, "and if what she told was true, why then I'll know ahead of time and the one *I* will charge is The Man With The Hammer." [5] Deciding, however, not to worry his mother, who is concerned over his fate, "he gave her his most docile smile, and snuggled his head against her, and she was comforted" (25).*

The basic device of this story is that of the fable, but Agee uses it with a difference. Most fables, depending on a heavy allegorization of isolated human traits, stress a moral to be learned about human behavior; in fact, the

---

* Page numbers in parentheses in this section refer to "A Mother's Tale," as reprinted in 23 *Modern Stories*. ed. by Barbara Howes. (New York: Vintage Books, 1963), pp. 3–25.

fable generally exists as a more or less schematized illustration of a specific moral, which already exists as a given outside the story itself. This is not true of Agee's story, which has no moral outside the resolution of the tension within the story. Also, Agee's characters do not stand for simple human characteristics: they are fully individualized as living human beings; their nature as cattle is accidental in that respect and only serves to provide Agee with an image for the human condition. The mother cow, for instance, is a typical portrait of a gentle, worried mother wishing the best for her children and trying to shield them from some of the dangers of life. She tries to evade her son's questions as long as possible but is forced into answering. "And hearing him, she knew that she would stop at nothing to bring that curiosity and eagerness, and that tendency toward skepticism, within safe bounds" (8). She knows that with children it is a bad policy not to answer questions: "She always tried hard to be a reasonably modern mother. It was probably better, she felt, to go on, than to leave them all full of imaginings and mystification" (6). Having explained what a wonderful life her son and the other calves would have staying home with her, "she looked happily and hopefully from one to another" (7).

The young calf also is individualized, as a young, impatient, reckless idealist. He is immediately enchanted with the idea of going out on the range (5); he asks his mother all the questions he can think of, and, in the end, he decides not to trust her, but to go and see for himself.

Although the characters may be identifiable as certain "types," they refuse to conform to the rigid allegorization of the usual fable. Primarily, this individualization is achieved through dialogue and through a sensitive outlining of the relationships between the characters:

"I want to go," she heard her son say with ardor. "I want to go right now," he cried. "Can I, Mama? *Can* I? *Please?*" And looking into his eyes, she was overwhelmed by sadness.

"Silly thing," she said, "there'll be time enough for that when you're grown up." (7)

Agee sensitive care in avoiding the rigidities of the allegorical form also characterizes his use of another basic (and time-worn) device, the use of the train journey as a symbol for the progression of life. Note, for example, how effortlessly, almost casually, he manages, without ever straining the verisimilitude of the tale, to suggest the shifting pace and sudden surprises of life:

But there was no food and no water, so they just had to put up with this; and about the time they became resigned to going without their suppers . . . they heard a sudden and terrible scream which frightened them even more deeply than anything had frightened them before, and the train began to move again, and they braced their legs once more for the jolt when it would stop, but this time, instead of stopping, it began to go fast, and then even faster, so fast that the ground nearby slid past like a flooded creek and the whole country, he claimed, began to move too, turning slowly around a far mountain as if it were all one great wheel. And then there was a strange kind of disturbance inside the car, he said, or even inside his very bones. He felt as if everything in him was *falling*, as if he had been filled full of a heavy liquid that all wanted to flow one way, and all the others were leaning as he was leaning, away from this queer heaviness that was trying to pull them over, and then just as suddenly this leaning heaviness was gone and they nearly fell again before they could stop leaning against it. He could never understand what this was . . . (10)

When the cattle have arrived at their destination and
been fed and watered, they begin to wonder about their
journey. Some of them, "the simple and ignorant," assume
a platonist point of view and begin "to wonder whether
that whole difficult journey, or even their whole lives up
to now, had ever really been. Hadn't it all been just
shadows, they murmured, just a bad dream?" (14) Others
try to see a Christian Providence in what has happened:

Even the sharp ones, who knew very well it had all really happened, began to figure that everything up to now had been
made so full of pain only so that all they had come to now
might seem all the sweeter and the more glorious. Some of the
oldest and deepest were even of a mind that all the puzzle and
tribulation of the journey had been sent us as a kind of harsh
trying or proving of our worthiness; and that it was entirely
fitting and proper that we could earn our way through to such
rewards as these, only through suffering, and through being
patient under pain which was beyond our understanding; and
that now at the last, to those who had borne all things well,
all things were made known: for the mystery of suffering
stood revealed in joy. (14)

This remarkable passage not only echoes the preface of
the Catholic Mass ("Vere dignum et justum est," or, in
The Book of Common Prayer, "it is meet and right") as
well as Biblical language in general ("beyond our understanding," "all things were made known," "the mystery
of suffering stood revealed in joy"), but it also associates
to the tribulations of Job, thus reinforcing the basic image
of the story, which is that of victims in a hostile universe.[6]
The journey also leads to two different but deeply
human emotions. The first is the solidarity with the race,
an experience of the brotherhood of all men:

. . . a new kind of strong and gentle delight, at being so very close, so deeply of his own kind, that it seemed as if the very breath and heartbeat of each one were being exchanged through all that multitude, and each was another, and others were each, and each was a multitude, and the multitude was one. (15)

The second experience is the realization of the absolute separateness and uniqueness of each individual:

. . . this wonderful knowledge of being one with all his race meant less and less to him, and in its place came something still more wonderful: he knew what it was to be himself alone, a creature separate and different from any other, who had never been before, and would never be again. (16)

It is part of the deep irony of the story that these two exhilarating and dignifying experiences should come immediately before the vicious encounter with The Man With The Hammer.

The device of having the mother retell the story of The One Who Came Back rather than having somebody experience the journey to the slaughterhouse first-hand is motivated, of course, by the desire to present that experience as a problem the others must come to terms with. For this is the theme of the story, and in this context The One Who Came Back assumes the function of one who returns to his kind to reveal eternal truth, almost like a Christ figure. His statements have the simplicity and rhetorical effectiveness of Biblical sayings. "For if even a few do not hear me, or disbelieve me, we are all betrayed" (22). Or:

All who are put on the range are put onto trains. All who are put onto trains meet The Man With The Hammer. All who stay home are kept there to breed others to go onto the range, and so to betray themselves and their kind and their children forever.

We are brought into this life only to be victims; and there is no other way for us unless we save ourselves. (22)

Thus, the theme of "A Mother's Tale" is the same as that of *Let Us Now Praise Famous Men*, "certain normal predicaments of human divinity," [7] the difficulty of accepting a life which consistently and viciously traps and destroys human beings. The basic image of mankind as cattle is not a result of the fabulist's need for ironic detachment but symbolizes mankind as victimized in a senselessly brutal world.

For the mother, the problem resolves itself in her love for her child and the awareness of purpose that this brings:

. . . they all looked at her at once in such a way that she loved her child, and all these others, as never before; and there dilated within her such a sorrowful and marveling grandeur that for a moment she was nothing except her own inward whisper, "Why, *I* am one alone. And of the herd, too. Both at once. All one." (23)

For her son, the problem resolves itself into a desire, idealistically and egotistically, to see for himself and, if what he has heard is true, to charge The Man With The Hammer in rebellion: "I'll put Him and His hammer out of the way forever, and that will make me an even better hero than The One Who Came Back" (25).

Above all, the problem is solved imaginatively in the writing of the story itself. For the ruthlessness and violence of the view of the world in the story are partly mitigated by the writer's compassion and understanding in relation to his characters. This is shown in Agee's use of a device which, in a review of André Malraux's film *Man's Hope*, he once called "excess of energy":

By excess of energy I mean his interest . . . in letting things and movements into his frame which have nothing to do with the central action or which enhance it only queerly and surprisingly—a guerrilla's sudden skipping change in step and his sudden hand to his sweating neck; or a dog wandering in from one corner of a street scene while a ball maunders in from another—little things which brilliantly lock men and their efforts and feelings into the exact real place and time of day.[8]

There are several examples of this device in the story. Listening to his mother's tale about the train journey, the young calf is given a sudden focus: "*Car*, her son said again to himself, How he would never forget the word" (9). This sentence illuminates the character of the calf not because it is relevant to the story, but exactly because it is irrelevant and alive. Similarly, describing the appearance of The One Who Came Back, the mother comments that "they say there is no imagining how terrible and in some way how grand the eyeball is when the skin has been taken entirely from around it" (20). This comment adds nothing to the narrative as such; it is an illustration which is convincing exactly because its irrelevancy is so entirely human. When the mother has just reassured one of the other calves that her tale is just an old legend, "all at once she was overcome by a most curious shyness, for it occurred to her that in the course of time, this young thing might be bred to her" (24). This comment, too, which is irrelevant to the basic vision of the story, becomes a glorification of the human in contrast to the inhumanity of the main theme. For added emphasis Agee even concludes the story with such an instance:

The littlest and youngest of them was doing double skips efforts to keep up with her. Now that he wouldn't be interrupting her, and none of the big ones would hear and make fun of him, he shyly whispered his question, so warmly moistly ticklish that she felt as if he were licking her ear.
"What is it, darling?" she asked, bending down.
"What's a train?" (25)

Thus, such "excesses of energy" function on two levels: first of all, they make the story go beyond the rigidities of the formal demands of the basic allegorical fable form; secondly, the irrelevancy and contrast of their content in relation to the rest of the story serve as an affirmation of faith in the face of overpowering reason. If the story suggests, on one level, that life is brutal and a senseless slaughtering of victimized mankind, it affirms, on another level, the beauty, glory, and delight of life, although these may seem irrelevant to all logic. And since it is this illogical sense of affirmation which dominates the tone of the story, it exists in tension with the basic image, not just in the isolated instances quoted but throughout. Similarly, the treatment of cattle as human beings (in characterization) becomes itself an affirmation that a human being can rise above his condition as victim and become a thing of grandeur and glory: "Be not like dumb-driven cattle, be a hero in the strife" (24).

2

Some of the most exciting and brilliant prose ever written in American literature can be found in *The Morn-*

ing Watch and *A Death in the Family*. Agee's prose has that exclusive touch of magic which makes it all but impossible to analyze in strictly objective terms. Primarily, its function is descriptive, as in the following passage:

They turned aside into a darker street, where the fewer faces looked more secret, and came into the odd, shaky light of Market Square. It was almost empty at this hour, but here and there, along the pavement streaked with horse urine, a wagon stayed still, and low firelight shone through the white cloth shell stretched tightly on its hickory hoops. A dark-faced man leaned against the white brick wall, gnawing a turnip; he looked at them low, with sad, pale eyes. When Rufus' father raised his hand in silent greeting, he raised his hand, but less, and Rufus, turning, saw how he looked sorrowfully, somehow dangerously, after them. They passed a wagon in which a lantern burned low orange; there lay a whole family, large and small, silent, asleep. In the tail of one wagon a woman sat, her face narrow beneath her flare of sunbonnet, her dark eyes in its shade, like smudges of soot. Rufus' father averted his eyes and touched his straw hat lightly; and Rufus, looking back, saw how her dead eyes kept looking gently ahead of her.[9]

As description, this passage is clear and precise at the same time that it is suggestive enough to give an impression of Rufus's point of view. Market Square is presented in visual images: the pavement is streaked with urine, a low firelight shines in a wagon, in another wagon the light shines "low orange," the woman's face is "narrow beneath her flare of sunbonnet," her eyes are "smudges of soot." Yet, at the same time, the mystery of a dark street in a city is presented to the child's eyes in images that are primarily emotional: in the dark street, the faces look "more secret," the light is "odd, shaky," the dark-faced man has "sad, pale eyes," he looks at them "sorrowfully, somehow dangerously," the woman's "dead eyes kept looking gently ahead of her." Thus, the passage admits the reader to a dual perspective: it lets him see Market Square as it is, at night, and, at the same time, affords him an insight into Rufus's mind.

The remarkable thing about Agee's prose is its enormous flexibility. It has a basically smooth and, above all, "American" sense of rhythm:

Rufus seldom had at all sharply the feeling that he and his father were estranged, yet they must have been, and he must have felt it, for always during these quiet moments on the rock a part of his sense of complete contentment lay in the feeling that they were reconciled, that there was really no division, no estrangement, or none so strong, anyhow, that it could mean much, by comparison with the unity that was so firm and assured, here.[10]

In this sentence, the placing of such modifiers as "at all," "really," "anyhow," and "here" gives the prose a smooth, almost conversational, flow which is distinct from the often clipped rhythm of British writing; and in the last part, the almost casual tacking-on of clauses imitates the mental processes of slowly emerging afterthoughts. Occasionally, this precise and yet sensitive prose slips into the rhythm and diction of the American vernacular:

He unbuttoned the top buttons of his trousers and spread his knees, squatting slightly, to hold them up. Fool thing to do, he reflected. Do it every time. (He tucked in the deep tails and settled them; the tails of this shirt were particularly long, and this always, for some reason, still made him feel particularly masculine.) If I put on the shirt first, wouldn't have to do that fool squat.[11]

Without burlesquing the Southern accent, this simple imitation of the natural speech rhythm and syntax establishes a familiarity with the character. On other occasions, Agee's prose moves in the opposite direction, toward a highly intense mode of writing which is capable of carrying strong symbolism at the same time that it describes, accurately and vividly, the perception at its center:

Tied in its white veil, stifled, a huge masked Head, a thinly clouded Sun, the monstrance stood from the top of the tabernacle and broke at its center a dense tissue of flowers and light: candles it seemed by thousands, spear-high and merely tall, and short, and guttering, each an abiding upright fiery piercing and, crisp and wearying, withering, dying, the frugal harvest of the dawn of the year: from faint orchards the last apple blossoms, still tenderly raveling their slow-borne blizzard; branches of mild-starred dogwood and of the hairy wild azalea, pink and white, from the mulled gray woods, and little fistfuls of those breathless violets which break the floor of winter, even the rare mayapple, the twin-leaf, whose bloom stays just a day; and, of the first shivering domestic flowers, cold jonquils, crowds of them, greenish with chill or butter yellow or flaming gold, and clear narcissus, reaching, bowing, staring, fainting in vases and jars of metal and glass and clay and in drinking glasses and mason jars and in small and large tin cans, all these each in their kind and sufferance bore witness before God while they might.[12]

This passage, from *The Morning Watch*, is intensely descriptive: the number of adjectives, for instance, is almost staggering. Yet all the adjectives are well chosen, clear, and precise, and, above all, emphasize the visual impression of the scene. At the same time, the syntactic predominance of adjectives, which stress the static nature of the scene, helps to reinforce, by sheer numbers, the impression of the profusion of flowers as well as the confusion of conflicting impressions. Finally, for all its effectiveness as pure description, this passage, through its careful diction, suggests both late winter and early spring, the dying and the dawn of the year, and thus becomes a symbolic accompaniment to the death and resurrection of Christ, which is a dominant motif in the story as a whole.

On still other occasions, Agee's prose moves into a lyrical mode which, with such devices as alliteration and a subtle imitative sense of rhythm, suggests the distance of the scene from the heart of the narration and the difficulty of remembering the past as it was:

Now is the night one blue dew, my father has drained, he has coiled the hose.
Low on the length of lawns, a frailing of fire who breathes.
Content, silver, like peeps of light, each cricket makes his comment over and over in the drowned grass.
A cold toad thumpily flounders.
. . . .
Parents on porches: rock and rock: From damp strings morning glories: hang their ancient faces.
The dry and exalted noise of the locusts from all the air at once enchants my eardrums.[13]

Sometimes, this lyrical mode makes use of Biblical rhetoric to suggest that the child's dependance on his parents is similar to the metaphysical need for God:

I hear my father; I need never fear.
I hear my mother; I shall never be lonely, or want for love.

When I am hungry, it is they who provide for me; when I am in dismay, it is they who fill me with comfort.

When I am astonished or bewildered, it is they who make the weak ground firm beneath my soul: it is in them that I put my trust.

When I am sick, it is they who send for the doctor; when I am well and happy, it is in their eyes that I know best that I am loved; and it is towards the shining of their smiles that I lift up my heart and in their laughter that I know my best delight.

I hear my father and my mother and they are my giants, my king and my queen, beside whom there are no others so wise or worthy or honorable or brave or beautiful in this world.

I need never fear: nor ever shall I lack for lovingkindness.[14]

In the end, however, it is not just the use of the various devices of prose style which is important but rather the fact that the prose has a consistency of tone which makes it possible to move from one mode of writing to another without losing the sense of continuity. The importance of this will easily be seen in a more specific examination of *The Morning Watch* and *A Death in the Family*.

3

The story of *The Morning Watch* is simple and, in itself, uninteresting. A twelve-year-old-boy, Richard, wakes up on Good Friday morning, having against his will failed to stay awake in prayer all night. Together with two other boys, he goes to the school chapel, where he extends his participation in the morning watch to one hour instead of a half hour. After the watch, the three boys, disobeying their instructions, go swimming, Richard kills a snake, and they return for whatever punishment may be in store for them. The structure of the story conforms to the simple Aristotelian requirement of a beginning, a middle, and an end: before the watch, during the watch, and after the watch.

The theme of the story is Richard's gradual change from youthful inability to accept suffering and death to a more mature realization that these are inevitable components of the human condition. This theme is emphasized through certain basic motifs in the story. There is, first of all, the death and resurrection of Christ at Easter. Secondly, the death of God is associated with the death of Richard's own father six years earlier. Thirdly, the theme of death and rebirth is echoed in the images of nature in early spring: the flowers in the chapel are "the frugal harvest of the dawn of the year," which "break the floor of winter." [15] This motif is given added emphasis since, just as the story moves from sleep to waking, it also moves from the nervous quiet of the dormitory and the suffocating intensity of the chapel into the exhilarating freedom of the outdoors. Fourthly, Richard's dive into the dark water of the pool is in itself a baptismal symbol and, as such, is still another variant on the death—rebirth theme. Also, the empty locust shell which Richard finds is, again, a symbol of nature's ability to renew itself. Richard's merciful killing of the snake which has been attacked by the two other boys represents his acceptance of the fact that although nature is reborn, just as the snake "had just struggled out of his old skin and was with his first return of strength venturing his new one" (109–10),* death is finally inevitable and must recur over and over again, just as Christ's agony on

* Page numbers in parentheses refer, in this section, to *The Morning Watch* (Boston: Houghton Mifflin Company, 1951)

the cross not only occurred at a certain moment in history but also takes place, again and again, every Easter.

Thus, the story is, as J. S. Phillipson has pointed out in great detail,[16] a carefully integrated work in which "symbols and motifs act, interact, and interrelate complexly." [17] Phillipson is correct in saying that in "their ordered complexity" these symbols and motifs "contrast with the disorder and confusion within the mind of the book's protagonist." [18] But also, there are within the work itself a number of larger symbolic constructs which become particularly interesting viewed in the light of Agee's total career.

First of all, the work conforms in many ways to one of the most common of American themes, namely that of the initiation of the individual into the new world, particularly as described by R. W. B. Lewis:

. . . the proposition, implicit in much American writing from Poe and Cooper to Anderson and Hemingway, that the valid rite of initiation for the individual in the new world is not an initiation *into* society, but, given the character of society, an initiation *away from it:* something I wish it were legitimate to call "*de*initiation." [19]

In this journey from innocence to experience, Richard grows more and more alienated from the surrounding society. The experience in the chapel is crystallized into a willful act of disobedience when Richard leads the boys to the Sand Cut. The killing of the snake earns for Richard an unexpected respect from the others: "in putting his bare hand within range of that clever head and in killing so recklessly and with such brutality, he had lost their contempt and could belong among them if he wanted to"

(111). But this no longer seems as important as it did before; Richard refuses to bring the snake with him although he realizes that he is thereby losing esteem, and all the way home he follows the other two without ever becoming part of *their* community. Thus, Richard's new maturity involves, among other things, a realization of the uniqueness and loneliness of the individual over and against the society to which he belongs.

The fact that Agee used this theme, which embodies so eloquently the specifically American dialectic of innocence and experience, belongs, of course, primarily to the history of ideas rather than to the study of literature. Nevertheless, it is well to remember that the theme, in one form or another, recurs constantly in Agee's books. In *Let Us Now Praise Famous Men*, for example, the constant effort to perceive as accurately as possible the essential experience of another human being leads to the realization of that individual's absolute uniqueness and loneliness, set apart from the surrounding society. The subjective and impressionistic method of the film criticism is a result of the realization that reality demands, above all, a response in *human* terms, regardless of society. In "A Mother's Tale," the tragedy of existence is conceived in such terms that the individual must decide if he wants to be "like dumb-driven cattle," a member of the herd, or "a hero in the strife," not of the herd, but himself alone.[20] Finally, although the theme has only a minor function in *A Death in the Family*, it is clearly enough spelled out to have significance: Rufus's confrontation with death disrupts his sense of belonging to his parents and relatives, and, at the end, taking a walk with Andrew (as in the beginning he takes a walk with his father), he finds that he cannot even ask a simple question.

Another large symbolic pattern in *The Morning Watch* is due to the fact that Richard's religious problem is so similar to Agee's artistic problem. Richard's total effort is directed toward realizing, with absolute immediacy, the death of Christ, but most of the time he fails:

By trying hard he was able to restore whole to his mind the thorn-crowned image of his Lord, but now it was not as he had seen it in prayer beside his cot but was very little different from a pious painting he knew: the eyes rolled up in a way that seemed affected, and in his cold sickness the image meant little to him. (11)

In the chapel, instead of concentrating on the meaning of the sacred events, he indulges in self-pitying daydreams in which he sees himself as another Christ.[21] Only by realizing that his efforts are doomed to fail is he finally brought to the stage where prayer comes naturally:

O you are dying my dear Lord for me, his soul whispered, wondering, weeping. For me, and I can't do anything for you. I can't even comfort you, or speak to you, or thank you. O my Lord Jesus I can thank you. I can think about you. I can try to know what it is you are going through for me. For me and for all sinners. I can know that every sin I do big or no matter how little is a thorn or a nail or the blow of the hammer or even just a fly that teases and hurts you in your blood, crawling and tickling and sipping and eating at you in the hot day on the Cross with you unable to brush him away or even to move, and every good thing, or true thankfulness or thought of love must make it anyway a little less terrible to suffer. (85)

In this passage, Richard accepts, almost for the first time, the inevitability of his own failures and is able, therefore, to pray with perfect contrition. It is at that moment, when he has relinquished the total effort to experience what Christ experienced, that he is rewarded:

He opened his eyes in quiet wonder. It was indeed to him the the very day. Not just a day in remembrance, but the day. There stood His consecrated Body, veiled among fire and flowers, but also living, in the flesh, on this very morning, at this very moment, He was waiting; and He was now within His last hours.

He won't see the sun go down today. (86)

Richard tries to bring a moment from the past into his own present. This, of course, is also Agee's artistic ambition (and if one accepts the common statement about the book that "the material is all autobiography," [22] the analogy becomes even more convincing): as Richard tries to experience Easter as happening for the first time, so Agee tries to render Richard's experience as occurring here and now, within the context of his language. The attempt is, finally, doomed to fail. The experience of reading a book is always different in kind from the experience described. No matter how brilliantly descriptive the prose is, the experience itself is finally inaccessible, beyond the realm of language. Yet, when Richard stops struggling against his own failures, "he was also filled to overflowing with a reverent and marveling peace and thankfulness" (87). He experiences the paradox of whispering something to himself, yet making an image of something totally different which is just as meaningful simply because it is touched with the sacredness of the moment: "My cup runneth over, something whispered within him, yet what he saw in his mind's eye was a dry chalice, an empty Grail" (87). How this freedom from his inhibiting ambition and pride affects

Richard is made abundantly clear in the remarkable passage when Richard dives into the water; the scene is at once a parallel to Christ's death agony and a baptism to the new life:

O Lord let me suffer with Thee this day, he prayed, his lungs about to burst; and took hold more firmly. You got no right, his own voice silently told him, you got no right. . . . Then he knew that he had stayed down too long; too deep; he could not possibly reach the air in time. Good. That's fine. *For Thee!* he groaned. *No right! Get out!* he shouted silently. But even before he could command it or fully decide to command it his body was working it for him; his feet braced against a ledge, his knees bent, and he leapt upward through the brightening water with more strength than he had realized he had left although the water seemed interminably tall above him and he knew still that he would never reach the surface in time and cried to himself, *I didn't have the nerve!* and, *Anyhow I tried*, meaning at once that he had tried to stay down too long as an act of devotion and that he had tried to save himself from the deadliest of sins; and broke the surface in time, head back, gasping, feebly treading water, watching the streaming bruise-colored clamorous and silent whirling of the world and taking in air so deeply that his lungs felt as if they were tearing; and soon the world became stable and all of the coloring and discoloration cleared and stood up strongly through the top of the woods across the tracks and he could realize that except for the remote voices of the two boys and the still more remote voice of a bird the world itself was delicately silent and all the noise was within his own head, and was rapidly dying: all that he saw still twitched with his pulse and out of the woods, beating like a heart, the sun stood up. (104–105)

The point of this passage is that after taking his sense of failure to the utmost limit, that of attempted suicide,

Richard discovers a new world and a new joy in existence: the world is silent except for the noises he himself provides, and the sun is standing up; and he realizes almost casually that he could have died: *"Here I am!* his enchanted body sang" (106). In effect, he has been reborn just as Christ is shortly to be resurrected.

Although it is not explicitly stated in the book, one can suggest here that Richard's final discovery has implications for the artist. Despite Richard's failure to experience in meditation the death of Christ, he is rewarded with a similarly sacred experience once he lets go and stops forcing himself. In the same way, if Agee cannot reproduce with full authenticity the real world in words, he can at least project a world of meaning on the chaos of mute signs, and the resulting experience is just as significant as any other experience, simply because it partakes of the sacramental nature of experience in general. Whereas Agee earlier, in *Let Us Now Praise Famous Men*, seemed to rebel against the limited power of words to embody, *The Morning Watch* suggests that this limitation must be accepted just as Richard accepts *his* world.

The Morning Watch is, above all, the skillfully rendered account of the maturing of a young boy. But keeping in mind Agee's obsession with the problem of rendering, truthfully and accurately, the essence of human experience, it does not seem irrelevant to suggest that *The Morning Watch*, in this respect, continues the ambition from *Let Us Now Praise Famous Men* and "Dedication." [23]

4

The difficulty of discussing *A Death in the Family* is obvious: Agee never finished the work himself, and the italicized sections, for instance, which constitute about one fifth of the book, have been given their places by the editors. It is therefore impossible to know how Agee had planned to combine the basic narrative with the more lyrical pieces outside the logical time-span of the novel. Still, this difficulty is not as crippling as it might have been.

In many ways, *A Death in the Family* can be read and appreciated as an ordinary novel. As such, its theme is, as Dwight Macdonald succinctly puts it, "the confrontation of love, which I take to be life carried to its highest possible reach, and death, as the negation of life and yet a necessary part of it." [24] The story is as simple as it could possibly be, yet outlines one of the most human of all situations. A young father, Jay Follet, receives a telephone call and leaves his wife and two children to drive to his father's deathbed. The message turns out to be exaggerated, and Jay drives home, only to be killed in a one-car accident. The rest of the book shows us his widow and children trying to comprehend the event during the next days through the funeral.

To convey this story, Agee employs a shifting point of view. Often the focus is on Rufus, the six-year-old son, and consequently many of the characters are given only the traits they have in a child's eyes. Father Jackson, for instance, appears as a threat who has come to take the place of the dead father: he appears "almost as tall as Daddy," [25] and he sits in Jay's chair. Listening to his voice praying, the children instinctively sense his presence as a threat to their mother as well as a threat to their place in their mother's affection (earlier, of course, Mary has been presented as in danger of adopting a piously religious attitude as a defense mechanism):

. . . Father Jackson's voice shifted and lost a bit of its vibrancy, and for a moment he talked as rapidly in a circle, seeming to assure them that of course he did not at all mean what they had thought he meant, but only, that (and then the voice would begin to gather assurance); they must realize (and now it had almost its old drive); in fact; of course—and now he was back again, and seemed to be saying precisely what he had said before, only with still more authority and still less possibility of disagreement . . . They realized that there was something to which their mother and their great-aunt were devoted, something which gave their voices peculiar vitality and charm, which was beyond and outside any love that was felt for them; and they felt that this meant even more to their mother and their great-aunt than they did, or than anyone else in the world did. They realized, fairly clearly, that the object of this devotion was not this man whom they mistrusted, but they felt that although everything was better for their mother than it had been a few minutes before, it was far worse in one way. For before, she had at least been questioning, however gently. But now she was wholly defeated and entranced, and the transition to prayer was the moment and mark of her surrender. (295–298)

The remarkable thing about a passage such as this one is that Agee, without abandoning the simplicity of diction appropriate to the children's point of view, manages to suggest the complexity of their unspoken feelings as well as the true danger of the situation.

Several chapters are written from Mary's point of view, in a modified omniscient technique. One chapter moves from Jay to Mary in order to show the nature of their relationship. One chapter is an interior monolugue, by Jay's brother Ralph, who has a minor function in the book as a whole. Clearly it is not through a consistent point of view

* Page numbers in parentheses refer, in this section, to *A Death in the Family* (New York: McDowell, Obolensky, 1957)

that the novel tries to achieve its unity. Instead, it appears, as W. M. Frohock has suggested, that Agee's job, "as he had set it up for himself, was to feel his way into character after character." [26]

The basic metaphor of the book is implicit in the idea of going home. The book opens with Jay and Rufus walking home, in perfect contentment, from a moving-picture show; when it ends, Rufus is walking home with Andrew, but this time in bewildered silence: things have changed. In the meantime, Jay has gone home to see his dying father, but on his way home to wife and children has been taken away. Also, in one of the lyrical chapters outside the time-span of the story, Jay sits with his hand on Rufus's forehead and remembers his mother doing the same for him:

And before his time, before even he was dreamed of in this world, she must have lain under the hand of her mother or her father and they in their childhood under other hands, away on back through the mountains, away on back through the years, it took you right on back as far as you could ever imagine, right on back to Adam, only no one did it for him; or maybe did God?

How far we all come. How far we all come away from ourselves. So far, so much between, you can never go home again. You can go home, it's good to go home, but you never really get all the way home again in your life. . . .

Just one way, you do get back home. You have a boy or a girl of your own and now and then you remember, and you know how they feel, and it's almost the same as if you were your own self again, as young as you could remember. (94)

The idea of going home, with its implications of death as well as a return to childhood, pervades the whole novel; as Leslie Fiedler has pointed out, it underlies the nostalgic tone of the writing itself:

. . . a longing to recapture the seen-for-the-first-time, to re-live the child's sense of warm, safe involvement in love, to believe again that such security is immune from death and change, to be what we were before we felt the need to iden-tify ourselves.[27]

In fact, Agee makes several efforts to capture certain scenes with the immediacy and accuracy of the film com-era.[28] One such scene occurs when Rufus views his father's dead body. It begins with an over-all view: "There was his head, his arms; suit: there he was" (307). Then it moves into a number of close-ups:

The arm was bent. Out of the dark suit, the starched cuff, sprang the hairy wrist.

The wrist was angled; the hand was arched; none of the fingers touched each other.

The hand was so composed that it seemed at once casual and majestic. It stood exactly above the center of his body.

The fingers looked unusually clean and dry, as if they had been scrubbed with great care.

The hand looked very strong, and the veins were strong in it.

The nostrils were very dark, yet he thought he could see, in one of them, something which looked like cotton.

On the lower lip, a trifle to the left of its middle, there was a small blue line which ran also a little below the lip.

At the exact point of the chin, there was another small blue mark, as straight and neat as might be drawn with a pencil, and scarcely wider.

The lines which formed the wings of the nose and the mouth were almost gone.

The hair was most carefully brushed.   (308)

Later, while Rufus is kneeling, he listens to the priest's

long prayer, and Agee inserts the view from Rufus's perspective, much in the manner of a close-up:

Some of the tiles of the hearth which peeped from beneath the coffin stand, those at the border, were a grayish blue. All the others were streaked and angry, reddish yellow. (313)

In still another place, one can almost sense Agee's desperation at not having a tape-recorder at hand:

Uhgh—hy uh yu hy why uhy uh: wheek-uh-wheek-uh:
Ughh—hy wh yuh: wheek:
(now the nearly noiseless, desperate adjustments of spark and throttle and choke)
Ughgh—hyuh yuhyuh wheek yuh yuh wheek wheek wheek yuh yuhyuh: wheek:
(which she never understood and, from where she stayed now, could predict so well):
Ughgh—*Ughgh*—yuhyuh*Ugh* wheek yuh yuh *Ughgh* yuh wheek wheek yuhyuh: wheek wheek: uh:
(like a hideous, horribly constipated great brute of a beast: like a lunatic sobbing: like a mouse being tortured):
Ughgh—*Ughgh*—*Ughgh* (Poor thing, he must be simply furious) *Ughgh*—wheek—*Whughugh*uyuh—*Ughweek*yuh*uughgyugh*yuhyuhy a a a a a a a h h h h h h h R h R h R H . . . (40)

This is Jay starting his Ford at night, and the passage continues for another page. Such onomatopoetic exercises would be rather meaningless were it not that they testify to list everything seen and felt. To do this, the writer immediacy and every realistic detail included. That ambition, of course, goes beyond what is in the power of words to convey, and Agee shows that he is aware of this:

Rufus had come recently to feel a quiet kind of anticipation of the corner, from the moment they finished crossing the viaduct; and, during the ten to twenty minutes they sat on the rock, a particular kind of contentment, unlike any other that he knew. He did not know what this was, in words or ideas, or what the reason was; it was simply all that he saw and felt. (19)

The implication of this passage is that although human experience is so ineffable it cannot finally be rendered in words, the closest possible approximation would be simply to list everything seen and felt. To do this, the writer must necessarily go outside the awareness chosen for the point of view. This is especially apparent in the case of Rufus, for while Rufus has a clear notion of what he sees, he is too young to put into words what he feels. In the episode when Rufus goes shopping with Hannah, Agee's writing is certainly relevant to Rufus's experience, but it remains, in the end, descriptive and outside his mind:

There was no flurry and no dawdling as there would have been with any other woman Rufus knew; none of the ceremony that held his grandmother's shopping habits in a kind of stiff embroidery; none of the hurrying, sheepish refusal to be judicious in which men shopped. . . . Taken shopping with anyone else, Rufus suffered extreme boredom, but Hannah shopped much as a real lover of painting visits a gallery; and her pleasure clarified Rufus' eyes and held the whole merchant world in a clean focus of delight. If his mother or his grandmother was shopping, the tape which hung around the saleswoman's neck and the carbon pad in which she recorded purchases seemed twitchy and clumsy to Rufus; but in his great-aunt's company, the tape and pad were instruments of fascination and skill, and the housewives who ordinarily made the air of the stores heavy with fret and foolishness were like a challenging sea, instead, which his aunt navigated most deftly. (74–75)

Likewise, Rufus remembers the midwife who delivered him as "a glisten of gold and a warm movement of affection" (106). The long lyrical section describing Rufus's fear of the dark (80–85) goes so far beyond anything that could possibly be characterized as the child's awareness that it becomes, in effect, expressive of Agee's effort to move inside the experience rather than of the experience itself:

Darkness said:
When is this meeting, child, where are we, who are you, child, who are you, do you know who you are, do you know who you are, child; are you?
He knew that he would never know, though memory, almost captured, unrecapturable, unbearably tormented him. That this little boy whom he inhabited was only the cruelest of deceits. (84)

This theme, the search for identity, is first presented in the short sketch "Knoxville: Summer 1915," which was originally published in 1938 and is here used as a prologue:

We are talking now of summer evenings in Knoxville, Tennessee in the time that I lived there so successfully disguised to myself as a child. . . . After a while I am taken in and put to bed. Sleep, soft smiling, draws me unto her: and those receive me, who quietly treat me, as one familiar and well-beloved in that home: but will not, oh, will not, not now, not ever; but will not ever tell me who I am. (3, 8)

The image of the disquise suggests that the poet somehow exists outside time, returning only for the purpose of giving order and form (time) to the chaos surrounding him. In fact, Jay's realization that you can only go home through making a child is entirely analogous to the poet's ambition in making a poem: both are a means of projecting a world of meaning and identity, and in that sense there can be no *essential* distinction between the world of "reality" and the world of the poem.[29] The poem is, literally, the real world, just as the real world is a poem.

This breakdown of the distinction between art and life is one of the main themes in Agee's work as a whole, and in *Let Us Now Praise Famous Men* it is responsible for the intention to make the record "exhaustive, with no detail, however trivial it may seem, left untouched, no relevancy avoided, which lies within the power of remembrance to maintain, of the intelligence to perceive, and of the spirit to persist in." [30] Everything is significant. Everything has meaning, not because it necessarily contributes to the progression of the nominal subject or the novelistic story, but because it partakes of reality, and that, in itself, is implicitly meaningful. *A Death in the Family* is filled with what Agee called "excesses of energy," events and episodes that do not contribute markedly to the story of Jay, Mary, and Rufus, but that have their value in revealing what Edward Ruhe has called a "transfigured reality":

. . . this technically brilliant writing is above all quiet, reverent, modest, and uncannily accurate in reproducing a transfigured reality. Reality in this mode has a high degree of animation, a mysterious and miraculous life of its own. . . . a sacramental occasion evokes a sacramental style, marked by the extraordinary force of every grotesque and random detail, an implication of timeless significance suggesting some benignant apocalypse. [31]

The whole chapter dealing with Ralph at LaFollette, full of drink and self-pity, is, in this sense, irrelevant to the story of Jay and his death; but although it is irrelevant to Rufus, it is not irrelevant to Agee's attempt to "make" the total reality of his father's death (the assumption that the novel is autobiographical, based on, among other things, the fact that Agee's middle name was Rufus, and that his father died in an automobile accident when he was six years old, is not strictly necessary: the argument is equally valid if we presume the poet to be making a fictional world). The shopping expedition with Hannah and Rufus is likewise irrelevant to the *story*: it may illuminate the characters involved but not as they relate to the main action. Another example occurs when Rufus is looking at his father's empty chair:

With a sense of deep stealth and secrecy he finally went over and stood beside it. After a few moments, and after listening most intently, to be sure that nobody was near, he smelled of the chair, its deeply hollowed seat, the arms, the back. There was only a cold smell of tobacco and, high along the back, a faint smell of hair. He thought of the ash tray on its weighted strap on the arm; it was empty. He ran his finger inside it; there was only a dim smudge of ash. There was nothing like enough to keep in his pocket or wrap up in a paper. He looked at his finger for a moment and licked it; his tongue tasted of darkness. (281)

This straightforward statement of simple actions conveys beautifully Rufus's sudden experience of a sense of loss; but what makes it convincing is his act of licking his finger and tasting darkness. At the moment reality is transfigured, the significance of the act exceeds that of the "novelistic" event.

In many ways, the "meaning" of the novel is to be found in the relationship between the two basic levels of the narrative: the italicized episodes outside the time-span, and the story of the death itself. The vignettes, significantly, all take place before Jay's death, and they introduce several of the themes that occur in the central story. With only one significant exception (Jay's reflections on going home), they all assume Rufus's point of view and serve, in that sense, to define Rufus as a central awareness.

The first episode, Rufus's experience of darkness (80–96), suggests, as stated earlier, the poet's assumption of Rufus as a disguise in order to project some meaning on the chaos of experience. More importantly, Rufus's experience of darkness is a premonition of the death to come and reveals the terror with which that is regarded:

And somewhat as in blind night, on a mild sea, a sailor may be made aware of an iceberg, fanged and mortal, bearing invisibly near, by the unwarned charm of its breath, nothingness now revealed itself: that permanent night upon which the stars in their expiring generations are less than the glinting of gnats, and nebulae, more trivial than winter breath; that darkness in which eternity lies bent and pale, a dead snake in a jar, and infinity is the sparkling of a wren blown out to sea; that inconceivable chasm of invulnerable silence in which cataclysms of galaxies rave mute as amber.   (84)

When Jay comes in to console Rufus, this not only leads into the theme of going home, which is so central to the whole conception of the novel, but also asserts the family circle, the simple relationship of father and son, as a defense against the onslaughts of the universe. The home, located in time and space, is itself an image of order and meaning projected on nothingness.

The second episode elaborates on this theme in two significant ways. First, it establishes the *feeling* of home, the absolute presence of the parents as people who look, dress, talk, sing, and smell in certain specific ways:

His cheeks were warm and cool at the same time and they scratched a little even when he had just shaved. It always tickled, on his cheek or still more on his neck, and sometimes hurt a little, too, but it was always fun because he was so strong.
He smelled like dry grass, leather and tobacco, and sometimes a different smell, full of great energy and a fierce kind of fun, but also a feeling that things might go wrong. (101)

Significantly, Rufus does not feel any fear of the darkness of the universe in the presence of his parents: "looking up between their heads from where he lay he looked right into the stars, so near and friendly, with a great drift of dust like flour across the tip of the sky" (99).

Secondly, this episode presents an ironic variation on the theme by giving Rufus's reflections on the line "Coming for to carry me home" in the spiritual his parents are singing:

Home was a long, long way. Much too far to walk and you can only come home when God sends the cherryut for you. And it would care him home. He did not even try to imagine what home was like except of course it was even nicer than home where he lived, but he always knew it was home. He always especially knew how happy he was in his own home when he heard about the other home because then he always felt he knew exactly where he was and that made it good to be exactly there. (98–99)

This, again, is a premonition of death to come, of Jay's ironic journey home.

The third episode (102–11) shows Rufus confronted with another momentous event, the birth of his sister. The important thing here is the conflict between Rufus's natural curiosity and the unwillingness of his mother to tell him what is going on. His lack of comprehension and his confusion lead to a sense of alienation which is symbolically represented by the fact that he is sent away from home. His growing mystification is emphasized, again, in the conversation with Victoria, and he is saved from despair only by the human presence of Victoria, whose darkness, of course, is in ironic contrast to his previous experience: "A silence opened around them in which he felt at once great space, the space almost of darkness itself, and great peace and comfort; and the whole of this immensity was pervaded by her vague face and by the waving light of leaves" (110-111).

In the fourth episode (213–26), the theme of alienation is continued. Rufus sees an enviable community in the groups of boys and girls on their way to school, and he longs to be a member. The boys, however, despite their friendly appearance, continually tease him, and "it puzzled him very deeply" (28). He is unable to understand the purpose of their behavior:

If they knew his name all the time, as apparently they did, why did they keep on asking as if they had never heard it, or as if they couldn't remember it? It was just to tease. But why did they want to tease? Why did they get such fun out of it? Why was it so much fun, to pretend to be so nice and so really interested, to pretend it so well that somebody else believed you in spite of himself, just so that he would show that he was deceived once again, because if you honestly *did* mean it, this time, he didn't want to not tell you when you honestly seemed to want so much to know. (218)

His very frustration, of course, makes him even more eager to be part of their world: "The less he believed them, the more he was led to believe them, and the easier it was for him to believe them. The more alone he felt, the more he wanted to feel that he was not alone, but one of them" (219). The boys, however, came up with enough subtle variations on their game to keep him interested and to be able to continue to violate his trust in them.

The visit to Rufus's great-great-grandmother returns to the earlier themes. It shows, first of all, the continuity of life and places Rufus as the last link of a long chain, located in time and place, belonging somewhere. On the other hand, the old woman, almost destroyed by age, is also a reminder of imminent death: "vague light sparkled in the crackled blue of the eye like some kind of remote ancestor's anger, and the sadness of time dwelt in the blue-breathing, oily center, lost and alone and far away, deeper than the deepest well" (239). But it is when she returns to the present and smiles at Rufus that he suddenly feels a great love for her and kisses her again.

The last of these episodes, the train ride to the Smoky Mountains (241–46), is another variation on the theme of violated trust. Uncle Ted tells Rufus that if he whistles loud enough, the cheese will jump off the table. Rufus believes him, tries to whistle, but cannot understand why everybody is laughing at him. His mother comes to his defense:

He's a very bright child *indeed*, if you must know. But he's been brought up to *trust* older people when they tell him something. Not be *suspicious* of everybody. And so he trusted you. Because he *likes* you, Ted. Doesn't that make you ashamed. (246)

Here, again, Rufus is made to feel helpless in a situation he does not understand.

In the very real sense, the main story of *A Death in the Family* is simply a continuation of these episodes. The themes are brought together and crystallized when Jay dies. The security of the home is suddenly disrupted, and everything changes. On a gigantic scale, it is simply another instance of violated trust, an incident so enormous and mysterious that it is· beyond comprehension.

The basic difference lies in the use of point of view. The lyrical episodes all define Rufus's way of looking at the world; the main story moves between all the characters although its structure, beginning and ending with Rufus, gives a certain emphasis to the child's experience. One of the effects of this contrast between the two levels of narrative is an impression that the book has been written by Rufus grown up, in an attempt to understand what he could not understand as a child. But although this may be true, as a matter of biography, it is never made explicitly clear in the novel.

On the other hand, the shifting point of view implies that it is not the death itself, or even Rufus's attempts at comprehending it, which is the real theme of the novel. In terms of the unity of the book, in relation to the central event, the technique of shifting from one character to another is dangerously disruptive; either Rufus's or Mary's or Hannah's point of view would have been more desirable. But the point of the novel is actually the absolute incomprehensibility of the event; what remains is simply the perception of the trivial details of actual reality.

This is demonstrated in a number of passages. One of the most significant is Mary's suggestion of what to put on

Jay's gravestone, and her father's sudden realization of
what her effort actually means:

That's what they're for, epitaphs, Joel suddenly realized. So
you can feel you've got some control over the death, you
own it, you choose a name for it. The same with wanting
to know all you can about how it happened. And trying to
imagine it as Mary was. Andrew, too. Any poor subterfuge'll
do; and welcome to 'em. (174)

The long sequence at night, when Mary and her parents
and Hannah are told about the accident by Andrew, is an
agonizingly detailed effort to own the event, to give it
meaning simply by describing it. But the relief is only
temporary for Mary; she, too, encounters the timeless
darkness that Rufus saw as a child:

She lay straight on her back with her hands open, upward at
her sides and could just make out, in the subtly diminishing
darkness, a familiar stain which at various times had seemed
to resemble a crag, a galleon, a fish, a brooding head. Tonight
it was just itself, with one meaningless eye. It seemed to her
that she was falling backward and downward, prostrate,
through eternity; she felt no concern. (211)

Rufus, of course, fails completely to comprehend the
event, in the sense that he wants to:

Rufus listened to his mother's shattered breathing and gazed
sidelong past her fair shoulder at the sheet, rumpled, and at a
rubbed place in the rose-patterned carpet and then at something queer, that he had never seen before, on the bedside
table, a tangle of brown beads and a little cross; through her
breathing he began once more to hear the quarreling sparrows;

he said to himself: *dead, dead*, but all he could do was see and hear; the streetcar raised and quieted its grim, iron cry; he became aware that his cap was pushed crooked against her and he felt that he ought to take it off but that he ought not to move just now to take it off . . . (252)

Among other things, this is a statement on aesthetics. For if the event is finally beyond comprehension, the only thing that remains is to see and hear the world as it exists. In the end, *A Death in the Family* is a demonstration of the impossibility of comprehending death in human terms. Despite her attempts to own the event, Mary is not able to comprehend its meaning: like Hannah, she falls back on her faith, but even that cannot explain it in *human* terms. Andrew questions the whole event bitterly throughout; Catherine is too young even to come close to understanding it; and Rufus is left bewildered. Walking home with his uncle, he even fails to understand personal relationships that he previously took for granted:

He hates them just like opening a furnace door but he doesn't want them to know it. He doesn't want them to know it because he doesn't want to hurt their feelings. He doesn't want them to know it because he knows they love him and think he loves them. He doesn't want them to know it because he loves them. But how can he love them if he hates them so? How can he hate them if he loves them? Is he mad at them because they can say their prayers and he doesn't? He could if he wanted to, why doesn't he? Because he hates prayers. And them too for saying them. (338–339)

The death of Jay Follet does not clarify anything: it has no meaning, and nothing can give it meaning. The shifting point of view, among other things, simply emphasizes, in varying degrees, the limited nature of human comprehension; and the almost total failure of understanding the event itself as well as those surrounding it is neatly summed up in a short passage toward the end:

There they stayed quiet, the deceived mother, the false son, the fatally wounded daughter; it was thus that Andrew found them and, with a glimpse of the noble painting it could be, said to himself crying within himself, "It beats the Holy Family." (326)

Nor does Agee give the event more meaning than it has for the characters. In terms of the people involved, the novel is curiously static: they do not change and they do not develop. Death brings no sudden maturation; it simply changes their situations. Rufus is no wiser at the conclusion; on the contrary, he has lost whatever understanding he had of the world. There is no evidence that Mary learns to accept the world; on the contrary, despite her father's advice, she uses her religion as a crutch to lean on.

But the central meaning of the book is implied in Rufus's realization that if death cannot be comprehended, the only thing that remains to do is to see and hear the world. In the light of this realization, everything is significant, not because it is relevant to the matters at hand, but simply because it exists. If death cannot be comprehended, at least life can be affirmed. This is actually the dominant movement of the novel as a whole. The careful attention paid to all details and the love with which the world of the Follets is made explicit are in themselves a celebration of reality and as such an implicit answer to the question which is asked.

One can compare *A Death in the Family* with *Let Us Now Praise Famous Men*, in the oblique nature of the technique employed. The earlier book asked the question: How is it possible to comprehend the existence of another human life? And, coming to the conclusion that this is finally impossible, it succeeded, obliquely, in creating the presence of the writer. The novel asks the opposite question: How can one actually comprehend death? And while concluding that it is, finally, impossible, it asserts simply that the world exists. In the process of showing nothingness and death invading the world, that world has been created and celebrated. This world may be only fictional, but, in a deeper sense, this is insignificant, for the writer's response to his "material" is just as valid a human emotion even were that world real. What matters is not whether the world exists in a book or not; what matters is the response to it, and in that sense the world in *A Death in the Family* is the real world.

Leslie Fiedler has suggested that Agee's novel is really not a novel but a poem:

To attempt to translate the book's meaning out of its expression is to realize that, whatever its failure to achieve novel form, it is, in the full sense, poetry: an unanalyzable fusion of theme and image, significance and language. [32]

Obviously, such a statement depends on what definition of the novel it presupposes; Agee's book would fit quite nicely into Forster's definition of the novel as "any fictitious prose work over 50,000 words." [33] On the other hand, the reader who demands that in a novel the characters act in a certain way and that the action is given a significance above and beyond its meaning as action, through the various literary devices at the novelist's disposal, will find Agee's novel dissatisfying, eventless, perhaps dull, probably sentimental.[34]

But, as Fiedler suggests, the important thing is not whether or not the book *is* a novel, but that "it is, in the full sense, poetry." As poetry, however, it is different in *kind* from much that we usually mean by poetry. In Agee's book there is not only a fusion, for example, of significance and language; significance *is* language. It is not just a fusion of content and style but a total breakdown of the division between the two; as Edward Ruhe has suggested, "reality is so overwhelmingly the subject matter that questions of style drop out of sight."[35] The author's search for meaning occurs within the realm of language, but this is not a *symbolic* action; it is an action like any other. In this respect, Agee's aesthetic derives ultimately from Whitman, for whom, as Charles Feidelson has put it, a poem, "instead of referring to a completed act of perception, constitutes the act itself, both in the author and in the reader; instead of describing reality, a poem is a realization."[36]

It is impossible to know exactly what revisions Agee would have made had he lived to complete *A Death in the Family*. Still, it is worth noting that no matter how he might have changed the arrangement of the chapters outside the central story, the basic nature of the book itself would have remained unchanged. It is not in the chronological arrangement that the meaning of the work is to be found; rather, it is in the shifting point of view, in the sense of detail, relevant or irrelevant, and in the implicit recognition of language as reality, that the work declares its intention. Like Whitman, adding to *Leaves of Grass*, like Pound, writing new *Cantos*, Agee could have added on to *A Death in the Family* without losing the essential nature of the experience.[37] That he did not live to do so may be tragic, as it deprives us of literature that would have been rich and meaningful, but at least his novel remains, for all its fragmentary appearance, as one of the most remarkably original and carefully executed works of the twentieth century.

WRITE WHEN, ALL, AND WHAT YOU CAN

CONCLUSION

The standard opinions on James Agee's literary career divide rather neatly into two basic groups. The best, and most eloquent, spokesman for the first group is Dwight Macdonald, who, in his book *Against the American Grain*, places his comments on Agee together with essays on Mark Twain, James Joyce, and Ernest Hemingway under the heading "Heroes/Victims." Above all, he notes the failure which seems implicit in Agee's career. "Although he achieved much, it was a wasted, and wasteful, life. Even for a modern writer, he was extraordinary self-destructive." [1] Macdonald suggests that this very failure underlies the Agee cult: it is generally felt, he says, that Agee's life and personality "were at once a symbolic expression of our time and a tragic protest against it" and that, in this sense, what betrayed him was not weakness, but vitality.[2] Going further than popular opinion, he also suggests why American culture failed to make us aware of or accept Agee:

The times might have done better by Agee. They could exploit one or two of his gifts, but they couldn't use him *in toto* —there was too much there to fit into any one compartment. In another sense, American culture was not structured *enough* for Agee's special needs; it was overspecialized as to function but amorphous as to values. He needed definition, limitation, discipline, but he found no firm tradition, no community of artists and intellectuals that would canalize his energies. [3]

Macdonald's comments are certainly relevant to an understanding of Agee's career. But there is also in his lines a curious tone of resentment, a suspicion that perhaps Agee's failure was due not to his self-destructiveness but to *le trahison des clercs*, to the general failure of artists and intellectuals in the twentieth century. Macdonald, like, for that matter, Agee himself, seems to have expected from Agee the Great American Novel, and when that expectation was not fulfilled, his frustration became oddly personal:

I had always thought of Agee as the most broadly gifted writer of my generation, the one who, if anyone, might someday do major work. He didn't do it, or not much of it, but I am not the only one who expected he would. He really shouldn't have died, I kept thinking, and how this posthumous book makes me think it all the harder. [4]

"He really shouldn't have died": it is almost an accusation. Above all, it suggests that whatever Agee achieved in his own eyes, he did not live up to the promise *others* saw in him; and to make this the keynote of a literary evaluation is slightly odd.

The best spokesman for the second group is W. M. Frohock, who suggests that Agee was primarily a "craftsman" who gave himself completely to the job, whatever its literary merits:

His ability to plunge so deeply into a *Fortune* assignment was the first manifestation of what it was in Agee that has since made people say that he did not keep his "promise." Conventionally, if one writes a book of poems which "show promise" then one must go on and write another book of poems or the promise is not "kept." But Agee lacked, even more than other writers of our time, the traditional respect for genres. He went one step beyond Baudelaire's notion that any work of art contains an obstacle which the artist creates as part of the act of conceiving what he is going to do, and then conquers in the execution. For Agee, if not in theory at least in his practice of writing, the presence of an obstacle, in any kind of writing job whatever, was enough to give the job the status of a work of art. It would be false, of course, to say that he set as high a value on a *Fortune* article as on a poem or a piece of fiction, but it is gospel true that he could lose himself as completely in writing of one kind as in writing of the others. What counted was the job, the problem that was presented to the craftsman. [5]

Frohock goes on to wonder "just how much American talent is diverted in this way from the traditional literary forms?" [6] His question is reiterated by Robert Phelps, who, in his introduction of Agee's letters, wonders why, "when we look for masterpieces, we keep thinking in terms of novels and poems, when it may turn out that our truest, our subtlest uses of the word have gone underground and borrowed other less official forms." [7] Phelps, echoing Frohock, goes on to suggest that "nothing that Agee wrote in conventional forms" is more expressive of his temperament than "what. he managed to do with his film column in *The Nation*" or in his letters.[8]

Both Frohock and Phelps try to justify Agee on the grounds that his creative energy sought outlets not commonly accepted by the literary establishment. In this ambition they are joined by, among others, Alfred Kazin, who sees Agee as "a natural literary craftsman, not a literary intellectual," who "actually did better in popular and journalistic media—where certain objective technical requirements gave him a chance to create something out of his immense tenderness and his sense of comedy—than when he let himself go in purely speculative lyricism." [9]

A healthy antidote to both of these basic opinions on Agee's career is John Updike's thoughtful and intelligent review of the letters. Objecting to the present glorification of failure, the tendency to place such exaggerated demands on the function of literature that failure, and the admission of failure, can become the only logical ambition of the serious artist, Updike, daringly, suggests that Agee should be judged on the basis of his literary works only, and that these are considerable enough to ensure his reputation. Updike goes even further in suggesting Agee's specific limitations and talents:

Ideas—particularly the American idea of the Great Novel, literature as a Puritan Absolute—obsessed Agee, and hounded him out of contentment with his genius, which was for spontaneous, gregarious commentary rather than patient eremitical invention. [10]

In other words, Updike suggests, with his immoderate— and, Macdonald would say, self-destructive—tendency to *talk* too much and to plan, forever, "the kind of books, rife with Great Ideas, that a *Time* reviewer would judge 'important,'" Agee was, in fact, "not badly suited to working for Henry Luce." [11]

Obviously, all these views are, to varying degrees, relevant. It is impossible to deny, for instance, that Agee's life was, in the traditional sense, wasted. Instead of writing novels or directing movies, the two things that might have made him a "success," he spent almost all of his working years in the service of popular journalism. But then, if Agee's life was wasted, so was Blake's, with its almost fanatic concentration on versified prophecies which, in the minds of many, are hard to justify even now. So was Joyce's life, concluding with an almost incomprehensible seventeen-year assault on the nature of language itself. So, for that matter, was that of any serious artist who ever refused to conform to the values, artistic or non-artistic, embraced by the society which sat in judgment on his talents: Melville, Gauguin, and, to a certain extent, F. Scott Fitzgerald are other examples. The accusation of waste in Agee is, in fact, only symptomatic of the assumption among some modern critics that, in this enlightened age, a serious artist should succeed in his own lifetime.

Likewise, it is undeniably true that Agee found delight (mixed, of course, with agony) in the simple craft of writing. He could write as many as thirty drafts of one short paragraph for a cover story in *Time*, often changing only a word or two from one version to the next. But to offer this as a justification of his career is almost as meaningless as suggesting, in the first place, that his career was wasted. One view is simply the opposite of the other; and both are essentially historical statements, efforts to explain why he did not write the brilliant novels he did not write. In effect, both views are equally presumptuous in suggesting that he should or should not have lived his life in a certain way. In critical terms, it is a matter of historical fact that he lived his life the way he did, and no justification is needed. What counts is the work he did, and if this is studied attentively enough it will reveal, for those who need it, the justification of his career.

Finally, John Updike's notion that Agee's talent was "for spontaneous, gregarious commentary," that this made him well suited for journalism, and that, in this sense, he talked his life away, has strong elements of truth in it. Macdonald's personal testimony is only one among many:

He was always ready to sit up all night with anyone who happened to be around, or to go out at midnight looking for someone: talking passionately, brilliantly, but too much, drinking too much, smoking too much, reading aloud too much, making love too much, and in general cultivating the worst set of work habits in Greenwich Village. [12]

But both Updike and Macdonald fail to see that all the talking is only a variant of that personal communication which is the basic character of all he wrote. Walker Evans has suggested that "Agee did a great deal of writing in the air" and that "he talked his prose, Agee prose." [13] This is almost literally true, for nearly all of Agee's published works strive for the effect of absolute immediacy and try to induce in the reader an awareness that the work at hand is not artificial and "made" but simply one human being talking to another.

Certainly, in conventional terms, all this talking was time-consuming and wasteful, and so was the journalism. Agee was the first to admit this, but he also saw that every job could be bad for the writer:

As for the badness of the writer teaching, I agree all the way; I also think but am not perfectly sure, that there is no job on earth that is not bad for the writer; including writing; and that he who must earn a living has got to take the disadvan-

tages of any job for granted, and seek what advantages in
each he can find. Again, though: every job is bad for him, but
floating on blood-money can be even worse; killing. There
really is no answer or solution and for want of one must say,
live as you can, understand all you can, write when, all, and
what you can. [14]

This was written in a letter to Father Flye in 1934 when
Agee was twenty-five years old, but it is the significant
ambition behind his career as a whole and behind the
individual works. The implication is that the writer must,
first of all, live a full life as a human being, trying to ex-
tend his understanding of reality as far as possible. Once
this is done, it becomes possible, no matter what the
medium, at least to try to convey in words the ineffable
essence of the human situation.

Not everybody may agree with Agee's conception of
the writer's duty, but it is the background against which
all his works can be seen and evaluated. In part, it also
accounts for the strong element of autobiography in everything he wrote. The poetry, as this study has tried to show,
is perhaps no more personal than most poetry, with one
notable exception. The long prose poem "Dedication"
lists by name a number of Agee's relatives, friends, and
teachers. This radically subjective method is a device
contributing to the effort of breaking down the distinction
between art and life and depicting in art the world as
real rather than as fiction. In this ambition, Agee has a
predecessor in Walt Whitman (whom he acknowledges in
the poem itself), whose statement that "the United States
themselves are essentially the greatest poem" indicates the
kind of aesthetic that Agee followed all his life.

In "Dedication," the Whitman influence is mixed with a

strongly Christian world picture. This is even more notable in the rest of the poetry. But if one distinguishes between the kind of religious poetry which deals with religion and basically religious emotions and the kind that merely presupposes a religious structure of the world in dealing with an essentially human situation, Agee's poetry falls in the second category. The twenty-five sonnets, for example, are not religious outpourings of a devout poet; instead, they try to define, as accurately as possible, the human condition within the Anglo-Catholic framework. This contrast between the Anglo-Catholic world picture and the adoption of Walt Whitman as poetic model is typical of Agee's works, which so often exist between the two poles of revealed truth and the subjective experience of that truth.

Let Us Now Praise Famous Men is autobiographical in the same sense that "Dedication" is: Agee exists in the book, not as that abstract entity, "the author," but as James Agee, poet, journalist, and human being. In his effort to present the lives of certain people as inescapable human reality, Agee breaks down the distinction between art and life by not only presenting certain material but also talking about the aesthetics of his undertaking and the fallacy of supposing that human lives can ever be "material" for any kind of writing. Thus, the book as a whole becomes an extension of Baudelaire's notion that, as W. M. Frohock explains it, "any work of art contains an obstacle which the artist creates as part of the act of conceiving what he is going to do, and then conquers in the execution." [15] *Let Us Now Praise Famous Men* is only nominally a book about three tenant families in Alabama; essentially, it is the record of a struggle between life and art, between the desire to immortalize a segment of human reality and the fact that this cannot be done by any art. It is this struggle which exists as "an effort in human actuality"; [16] and the struggle is won only with the realization that the endeavor is finally hopeless and also meaningless. In the end, although the artistic ambition meets with failure, the recognition of this failure becomes the most moral (and human) thing to do, and since the book constantly declares exactly those values to be infinitely superior to those of art, the work is brought to a successful close.

This deeply original work has always been accused by critics of being formless and chaotic; but if Agee ever was formless, he had a purpose for it. In effect, *Let Us Now Praise Famous Men* has a carefully designed structure which constantly stresses the urgency and reality of the struggle with human experience. One reason why this structure has been so largely overlooked, apart from the radical innovation of the method in general, may be that it tries, in the simplest ways possible, to approach the kind of symmetry (and asymmetry) which Agee saw in the tenant farmer's simple pine-board shack. The complexity of Agee's struggle with the nominal subject matter *seems* to obscure the classical dramatic structure of the work.

Agee's film criticism for *The Nation* is equally subjective. As has been shown previously, this, too, was the result of a calculated effort. If the distinction between art and life is broken down, the function of the critic becomes simply to respond to the given work in straightforward human terms. The terms available to such a critic then hinge constantly on the requirement that the work of art be faithful to human reality. This is not a demand for a superficial realism, but an insistence that human reality, in all its forms, should be honored and respected for what it is and not abused into shallow artifice.

Agee loved the cinema as a medium because it had the ability to picture the real world more faithfully than perhaps any other medium: it could present the world with absolute objectivity, something impossible to do with words. But whereas Agee, as writer, tried to make his words transcend their inherent limitations, the motion-picture camera presented the opposite challenge. The world exists as the given for the camera, and the task is above all to honor it instead of just reproducing it, to capture the luminous moments of pure poetry which exist in the simplest object. For the critic, the camera's absolute fidelity presented a demand for a human response; and Agee's criticism is consistently subjective, impressionistic, and "human," rather than objective, scholarly, and "literary." Above all, the style of his weekly columns is distinctly personal and establishes, beyond doubt, the presence of the writer in every word.

The film scripts that Agee wrote, for himself as well as under contract, try, in varying degrees, to fulfill the requirements he set up as a critic. There are numerous examples of his ability to bring out in simple details the kind of fusion of fiction and documentary reality that he embraced. For this reason, his scripts often violate the common Hollywood code of providing simple dialogue and a few camera directions: they provide extensive descriptions not only of the specific shots, camera angles, sound effects, and actors' movements, but also of the particular effect to be gained from the whole. At times, these descriptions seem so specialized as to be of little use to a director and his crew; but this is simply the result of Agee's intense awareness of what he was after and what it was possible to achieve within the medium. Above all, they are a testimony to the abilities which might have made Agee a fine and intelligent director if he had ever been given a chance.

Agee's major fiction, the novella *The Morning Watch* and the posthumous novel *A Death in the Family*, continues the autobiographical trend in his works. Both can be shown to come straight out of his own childhood. This does not alter the essential value of the two works, but it lends added emphasis to an understanding of the nature of his aesthetics here. The attempt is made not only to describe and analyze a certain area of human experience, but also to present it to the reader. This ambition lies outside the realm which it is possible for words to control, and—just as in *Let Us Now Praise Famous Men*—the only possible alternative is to record, obliquely, the writer's struggle with his material. Thus, Agee's efforts to project meaning into the diversity of a certain segment of reality is the real and dramatic interest of *A Death in the Family*. The novel is not an analysis of a world perceived; it is the very act of perceiving it, or, if you will, the projection of meaning afforded by that perception.

There is something unmistakably American about Agee's life and works. Part of this is accounted for by the influence of Whitman's expansive sense of himself as a symbolistic writer or by a comparison with Melville, who started out as a successful promise, produced an unrecognized masterpiece, and retired into obscurity, not even bothering to publish his last work. But, more than this, it is the sense one has of Agee as a man using literature for private rather than public ends and often, in fact, insisting so strongly on his personal integrity as to defy all public expectations. This is the opposite of what has been called literature as institution; it is literature as a means of private discovery, and that notion certainly underlies the greatest of American writers: Whitman, Melville, Hawthorne, and Thoreau. As a phase of what R. W. B. Lewis has called the "*de*nitiation" from society it also appears in such modern writers as Hemingway, Faulkner, Bellow, and Salinger. (With the modern need for new words for old things, it is now often translated simply as alienation from society.)

One result of this private nature of American literature has been a remarkably open form or, as Hugh Kenner would call it, open field.[17] This is evident in the very flexibility of the American language, and it is equally evident in the unfinished form of so many American masterpieces. They seem to have been left "unfinished," simply to look ahead toward the future. Whitman's *magnum opus* existed in an embryonic stage and received innumerable additions in order to accommodate the passing of time, not in order to perfect a closed form already perceived as unified in its early version. Pound's *Cantos* have already gone far beyond any scheme that their author may have originally intended for them: they stand open to the future. Agee's *A Death in the Family* exists in much the same manner.

In this sense F. Scott Fitzgerald was correct when he complained that American lives have no third acts. Of course not; it is in the very nature of American experience to leave the third act unfinished, determined only by the future, and Fitzgerald is his own best example. And if the unfinished fragments seem to bring with them a charge of implicit failure, it is well to remember Melville's dictum that failure is the true test of greatness.

But if Agee is thus part of a well-defined American tradition, he is also typically modern in his insistence on the breakdown of the distinction between art and life. F.

W. Dupee has pointed out that "his main struggle was to recapture a creativity which he associated with Joyce, Griffith, Chaplin and others. He labored to represent a world that had been triumphantly realized by the modern masters." [18] It is also possible to point to such modern masters as Pirandello, Gide, Beckett, and the new French novelists, who have tried to define exactly the tenuous distinction between illusion and reality, art and life. This interest has made much of twentieth-century literature critical in nature: more than in previous centuries, the artist now appears in his own works, trying to provide a valid statement on aesthetics rather than on analysis of reality.

Agee differs from this ambition in that no matter how interested he was in exploring the limits of the art he was so passionately concerned with, he maintained a total and committed respect for reality as such. The conflict between art and life that he dramatized in work after work was geared to celebrate and praise the world as it is. To do this, he committed himself fully, as a human being, to the world, and it is in the end the greatness of his achievement that he lived as he could, understood all he could, wrote when, all, and what he could—and did it well.

NOTES

Chapter 1

[1] John Huston, "Introduction," *Agee on Film*, II (New York: McDowell Obolensky, 1960), p. ix.

[2] Macdonald, p. 144.

[3] Frohock, p. 215.

[4] *The Letters of James Agee to Father Flye* (New York: George Braziller, 1962), p. 37. Hereafter cited as *Letters*.

[5] *Ibid.*, p. 53.

[6] James Agee, *Permit Me Voyage* (New Haven: Yale University Press, 1934), p. 7.

[7] *New York Herald Tribune Book Review*, December 9, 1934, p. 19.

[8] *New York Times*, December 30, 1934, p. 10.

[9] *Saturday Review of Literature*, XL (November 24, 1934), 314.

[10] *Yale Review*, n. s. XXIV (Winter 1935), 394.

[11] Lincoln Kirstein, "New Potems," *New Republic*, LXXXII (February 27, 1935), 80.

[12] *Permit Me Voyage*, p. 6.

[13] *Letters*, p. 38.

[14] *Ibid.*, pp. 47–48.

[15] *Ibid.*, p. 55.

[16] *Harvard Advocate*, CXVII, no. 8 (May 1931), 9–23.

[17] "Vertigral," *Saturday Review of Literature*, XIV (September 5, 1936), 9.

[18] *Harvard Advocate*, CXVIII (February 1932). Reprinted in *The Harvard Advocate Anthology*, ed. Donald Hall (New York: Twayne Publishers, Inc., 1950), pp. 228–29.

[19] The second type, "two or more alternative meanings are fully resolved into one," as outlined by William Empson, in *Seven Types of Ambiguity* (New York: Meridian Books, 1958).

[20] *Harvard Advocate,* CXVI, no. 7 (April 1930), 25.

[21] *Letters,* p. 41.

[22] *Ibid.,* p. 47.

[23] Cf. such modern psychologists and philosophers as Erich Fromm, Carl Rogers, Martin Buber, and others, who claim that without a radical acceptance of the self it is impossible to approach the *world* with any kind of acceptance.

[24] *Letters,* p. 47.

[25] Yvor Winters, *In Defense of Reason* (New York: The Swallow Press and W. Morrow and Company, 1947), p. 512.

[26] Kirstein, p. 81.

[27] *Letters,* p. 34.

[28] R. W. B. Lewis, *The American Adam* (Chicago: The University of Chicago Press, 1959), pp. 49–51.

[29] Cf. Lewis, p. 49.

[30] Charles Feidelson, *Symbolism and American Literature* (Chicago: The University of Chicago Press, 1960), p. 18.

[31] Feidelson, *idem.*

[32] Lewis, p. 51.

[33] Walt Whitman, *An American Primer,* ed. Horace Traubel (Boston: Small, Maynard, 1904), p. 14. Quoted by Feidelson, p. 20.

[34] Feidelson, p. 20.

[35] Preface to 1855 edition, *Leaves of Grass,* ed. Emory Holloway, Inclusive edition (Garden City, N. Y.: Doubleday, 1925), p. 488. Quoted by Feidelson, p. 17.

[36] Feidelson, p. 18.

[37] *An American Primer,* pp. 16–17.

[38] *Letters,* p. 48.

[39] "Suburban Cawdor," *Harvard Advocate,* CXVII, no. 8 (May, 1931), 86–88.

[40] *The Complete Writings of Walt Whitman,* ed. Richard M. Bucke *et al.* (New York: G. P. Putnam's Sons, 1902), IX, 3.

[41] James E. Miller, *A Critical Guide to Leaves of Grass* (Chicago: The University of Chicago Press, 1957), pp. 256–261. For an acute study of the Whitman tradition in modern literature, see James Miller, Karl Shapiro, and Bernice Slote, *Start with the Sun. Studies in Cosmic Poetry* (Lincoln: The University of Nebraska Press, 1960).

[42] This is true even in grammatical terms: with a few exceptions the basic sentence structure in the poem is an incomplete sentence (to . . .), which, for its logical completion, *demands* a basis outside the poem itself.

[43] See Dorothy L. Sayers, *The Mind of the Maker* (New York: Living Age Books, 1959).

[44] Elizabeth Drew, *Poetry: A Modern Guide to Its Understanding and Enjoyment* (New York: Dell Publishing Co., Inc., 1959), p. 213.

[45] Drew, pp. 211–12.

[46] Agee's use of the child as an image of mankind recurs often; see, for instance, "A Song" in *Permit Me Voyage*, pp. 12–13, and "A Lullaby" in *One Hundred Modern Poems*, ed. Selden Rodman (New York: New American Library, 1949). pp. 100–101.

[47] *Letters*, p. 38.

[48] *Recognition of Robert Frost*, ed. Richard Thornton (New York: Henry Holt and Company, 1937), p. 294.

[49] John M. Bradbury, *Renaissance in the South* (Chapel Hill: The University of North Carolina Press, 1963), p. 186.

[50] *Ibid.*

Chapter 2

[1] *Letters*, pp. 104–105.

[2] *Ibid.*, pp. 114–115.

[3] *Time*, XXXVIII (October 13, 1941), 104.

[4] George Barker, "Three Tenant Families," *The Nation*, CLIII (September 27, 1941), 282.

[5] Harvey Breit, review in *New Republic*, CV (Sept. 15, 1941), 348–49.

[6] J. C. Cort, review in *Commonweal*, XXXIV (Sept. 12, 1941), 499–500.

[7] L. R. Etzkorn, review in *Library Journal*, LXVI (August 1941), 667.

[8] Ruth Lechlitner, "Alabama Tenant Families," *New York Herald Tribune Books* (August 24, 1941), p. 10.

[9] Paul Goodman, review in *Partisan Review*, IX, no. 1 (January-February 1942), 86–87.

[10] Quoted by Frohock, p. 218.

[11] Selden Rodman, review in *Saturday Review of Literature*, XXIV (August 23, 1941), 6.

[12] Macdonald, p. 158.

[13] "In Love and Anger," *Time*, LXXVI (September 26, 1960), 112.

[14] Granville Hicks, "Suffering Face of the Rural South," *Saturday Review*, XLIII (September 10, 1960), 19–20.

[15] Winfield T. Scott, review in *New York Herald Tribune Books*, (October 9, 1960), p. 6.

[16] Priscilla Robertson, "Agee's Special View," *The Progressive*, XXV (January 1961), 44–45.

[17] E. Larsen, "Let Us Not Now Praise Ourselves," *Carleton Miscellany*, II, no. 1 (Winter 1961), 86–96.

[18] Erik Wensberg, "Celebration, Adoration and Wonder," *The Nation*, CLXXII (November 26, 1960), 417–18.

[19] James Agee and Walker Evans, *Let Us Now Praise Famous Men* (Boston: Houghton Mifflin Company, 1960), p. xiv. Except for a larger selection of photographs and an added preface by Walker Evans, this edition is identical with the first edition of 1941.

[20] Cort, p. 500.

[21] Macdonald, p. 155.

[22] Wensberg, p. 418.

[23] Cf. W. K. Wimsatt, Jr., *The Verbal Icon* (New York: The Noonday Press, 1960), pp. 3–20.

[24] Breit, p. 348.

[25] Alfred Kazin, *On Native Grounds* (New York: Reynal and Hitchcock, 1942), p. 495n.

[26] Harold Rosenberg, *The Tradition of the New* (New York: Grove Press, 1961), p. 27n.

[27] *Ibid.*, p. 29.

[28] *Ibid.*

[29] *Ibid.*, p. 33.

[30] *Ibid.*, pp. 33–34n.

[31] *Ibid.*

[32] *Let Us Now Praise Famous Men*, p. 238n.

[33] Rosenberg, p. 29.

[34] Harold Rosenberg, "The New as Value," *The New Yorker*, XXXIX (September 7, 1963), 141.

[35] *Letters*, p. 84.

[36] Harold Rosenberg, "Insurrections," *The New Yorker*, XL (March 14, 1964), 180.

[37] Martin Buber, *Eclipse of God* (New York: Harper and Brothers, 1957), p. 126.

[38] Wensberg, p. 418.

Chapter 3

[1] *A Death in the Family* (New York: McDowell Obolensky, 1957), p. 12.

[2] *Letters*, p. 35.

[3] Macdonald, p. 160.

[4] *Ibid.*

[5] *Permit Me Voyage*, p. 17.

[6] *Letters,* p. 71.

[7] *Ibid.,* p. 89.

[8] *Let Us Now Praise Famous Men,* p. 234.

[9] *Agee on Film: Reviews and Comments* (New York: McDowell Obolensky, 1958), introduction. This volume is hereafter referred to as *Agee on Film,* I.

[10] Arthur Knight, review in *Saturday Review,* XLI (December 20, 1958), 9.

[11] Gerald Weales, "The Critic in Love," *Reporter,* XIX (December 25, 1958), 38–39.

[12] Jonathan Harker, review in *Film Quarterly,* XII (Spring 1959), 58–61.

[13] Arlene Croce, "Hollywood the Monolith," *Commonweal,* LXIX (January 23, 1959), 431.

[14] Richard Griffith, review in *New York Times Book Review* (November 16, 1958), p. 5.

[15] Bosley Crowther, review in *American Scholar,* XXIX (Summer 1960), 436.

[16] Winfield T. Scott, review in *New York Herald Tribune Book Review* (February 15, 1959), p. 12.

[17] Stanley Kauffmann, "Life in Reviews," *New Republic,* CXXXIX (December 1, 1958), 18–19.

[18] Norman Holland, "Agee on Film: Reviewer Re-Viewed," *Hudson Review,* XII (Spring 1959), 148–51.

[19] *The New Yorker,* XXXIV (December 13, 1958), 215–16.

[20] *Ibid.,* p. 216.

[21] Page references in parentheses refer, in this chapter, to *Agee on Film,* I.

[22] *Let Us Now Praise Famous Men,* p. xv.

[23] In this respect, Agee's criticism is strikingly similar to that of Manny Farber. For a representative example of Farber's criticism, see his "Underground Films," in *Film: An Anthology,* ed. Daniel Talbot (New York: Simon and Schuster, 1959), pp. 177–88. In their appreciation of unsophisticated "action" films, both Agee and Farber are forerunners of the presently fashionable "auteur" theorists; cf. Andrew Sarris, "The Auteur Theory," *Film Quarterly,* XVI (Summer 1963), 26–33. Sarris, in fact, has pointed out that Agee's essay on Huston is an "*auteur* piece," in "The American Cinema," *Film Culture,* no. 28 (Spring 1963), 30.

Agee himself mentions Farber a number of times only to point out that he finds himself in basic agreement with him (*Agee on Film,* I, 37, 118, 124, 155). Farber, on the other hand, in a review of *Agee on Film,* I, suggested that he did not care much for Agee's sophisticated writing in *The Nation* but much preferred his *Time* reviews of the "happy garbage" on the New York screens: "Star-Gazing for the Middlebrows," *New Leader*, XLI (December 8, 1958), 14–15.

[24] *Let Us Now Praise Famous Men*, p. 351.

[25] *Ibid.*, p. 357.

[26] *Ibid.*

[27] *The New Yorker*, XXXIV (December 13, 1958), 216.

[28] Holland, p. 148.

[29] *Ibid.*, p. 149.

[30] Cf. Harold Rosenberg, "Insurrections," p. 180.

[31] Robert Phelps, "James Agee," in *Letters*, p. 2.

[32] Kauffmann, p. 18.

Chapter 4

[1] Macdonald, p. 160.

[2] *Letters*, pp. 45–46.

[3] *Ibid.*, p. 199.

[4] *Ibid.*, p. 224.

[5] Farber, "Underground Films," in *Film: An Anthology*, pp. 177–88.

[6] *Ibid.*, p. 188.

[7] Erwin Panofsky, "Style and Medium in the Moving Pictures," in *Film: An Anthology*, p. 28. His italics.

[8] *Ibid.*

[9] *Ibid.*, p. 18.

[10] *Ibid.*, pp. 18–19.

[11] *Ibid.*, p. 19.

[12] *Ibid.*, p. 21.

[13] *Ibid.*

[14] *Ibid.*

[15] Vernon Young, "Film Chronicle," *Hudson Review*, XIV (Summer 1961), 275.

[16] For one exposition of the "auteur" theory in modern film criticism, see Andrew Sarris, "The Auteur Theory," *Film Quarterly*, XVI (Summer 1963), 26–33.

[17] Mark Schorer, "Technique as Discovery," *Forms of Modern Fiction*, ed. William Van O'Connor (Minneapolis: University of Minnesota Press, 1948), p. 16.

[18] George Bluestone, *Novels Into Film* (Baltimore: The Johns Hopkins Press, 1957), p. 5.

[19] Dudley Nichols, *Twenty Best Film Plays*, ed. with John Gassner (New York: Crown, 1943), p. xxxvi. Quoted by Bluestone.

[20] Jerry Wald, "Screen Adaptation," *Films in Review*, V (February 1954), 64. Quoted by Bluestone.

[21] James Agee, "Man's Fate," *Films*, I (November 1939), 60.

[22] Haakon Chevalier, "Translator's Introduction," in André Malraux, *Man's Fate* (New York: Modern Library, 1936), p. 1.

[23] *Agee on Film*, I, 237.

[24] Cf. *Let Us Now Praise Famous Men*, p. 240.

[25] Malraux, *Man's Fate*, p. 320.

[26] Malraux, *Man's Fate*, p. 323.

[27] *Agee on Film*, I, 240.

[28] *Ibid.*

[29] *Ibid.*, p. 241.

[30] Stephen Crane, *The Red Badge of Courage* and *Selected Prose and Poetry*, ed. William Gibson (New York: Holt, Rinehart and Winston, 1960), p. 214.

[31] *Agee on Film, Vol. II: Five Film Scripts* (New York: McDowell, Obolensky, 1960), p. 487.

[32] Crane, p. 214.

[33] *Ibid.*, p. 184.

[34] *Ibid.*, p. 488. For the image of the turning sky, cf. Agee's review of Rouquier's *Farrebique, Agee on Film*, I, 299.

[35] Crane, p. 187.

[36] Macdonald, p. 151.

[37] *Letters*, p. 185.

[38] Stephen Crane, *The Red Badge of Courage* and *Selected Prose and Poetry*, ed. William Gibson, p. 117.

[39] *Ibid.*

[40] Andrew Sarris, "The American Cinema," *Film Culture*, no. 28 (Spring 1963), 45.

[41] James Agee, "Notes for a Moving Picture: The House," in *New Letters in America*, ed. Horace Gregory (New York: W. W. Norton & Company, 1937), pp. 39–40.

[42] *Ibid.*, p. 37.

[43] *Ibid.*, p. 42.

[44] *Agee on Film*, I, 279.

[45] Notes for a Moving Picture: The House," p. 47.

[46] *Politics*, III (April 1946), pp. 121–25. Reprinted in *New Directions 10*, ed. James Laughlin (New Jersey: New Directions, 1948), pp. 252–63. Figures in parentheses on succeeding pages refer to this volume.

[47] This is not unusual in itself: all of Ingmar Bergman's scripts, for instance, are written in this manner.

[48] *The Letters of Wyndham Lewis*, ed. W. K. Rose (London: Methuen & Co., Ltd., 1963), p. 402.

[49] In the technique of its satire, "Dedication Day" is similar to

Stanley Kubrick's recent film *Dr. Strangelove, Or How I Learned to Stop Worrying and Love the Bomb.*

[50] *Agee on Film,* I, 239.

[51] *Agee on Film,* II, 8–9.

[52] *Ibid.,* p. 98.

[53] *Ibid.,* p. 20.

[54] Note for that matter, the abundance of plant and animal imagery in *Let Us Now Praise Famous Men.*

[55] *Agee on Film,* II, 6.

[56] *Ibid.,* p. 44.

[57] *Ibid.,* pp. 146–47.

[58] Richard Oulahan, "A Cult Grew Around a Many-Sided Writer," *Life,* LV (November 1, 1963), 70.

[59] *Agee on Film,* II, 77.

[60] *Ibid.,* p. 60.

[61] *Ibid.*

[62] *Ibid.,* p. 85.

[63] Vernon Young, "Film Chronicle," pp. 275–76.

[64] *Agee on Film,* I, 237.

Chapter 5

[1] *Letters,* p. 181.

[2] *Partisan Review,* XVIII (March 1951), 137–66; 206–31.

[3] *Harper's Bazaar,* LXXXVI (July 1952), 66–68; 102–107. Reprinted in *23 Modern Stories,* ed. Barbara Howes (New York: Vintage Books, 1963), pp. 3–25. Page references in the future refer to this edition.

[4] *Letters,* pp. 170–71.

[5] "A Mother's Tale," p. 25.

[6] The image works in two basic ways. First, there is obvious in the story a great deal of compassion for the cattle as such and an implied criticism of the human treatment of animals. (Cf. in this connection, *Letters,* pp. 229–32.) This aspect both reinforces and goes against the second implication of the image, which is the view of mankind as victims in a hostile universe (the association with the transportation of Jews to the gas chambers is not irrelevant here). Thus, by setting up the analogy that cattle are to men what men are to *their* fate, the symbolism becomes more effective.

[7] *Let Us Now Praise Famous Men,* p. xiv.

[8] *Agee on Film,* I, 240.

[9] *A Death in the Family* (New York: McDowell Obolensky, 1957), p. 15.

[10] *Ibid.*, p. 19.

[11] *Ibid.*, p. 30.

[12] *The Morning Watch* (Boston: Houghton Mifflin Company, 1951), pp. 26–27.

[13] *A Death in the Family*, p. 7.

[14] *Ibid.*, pp. 82–83.

[15] *The Morning Watch*, p. 27.

[16] J. S. Phillipson. "Character, Theme, and Symbol in *The Morning Watch, Western Humanities Review*, XV (Autumn 1961), 359–67.

[17] *Ibid.*, p. 359.

[18] *Ibid.*

[19] R. W. B. Lewis, *The American Adam*, p. 115.

[20] "A Mother's Tale," pp. 22–24.

[21] Cf. Phillipson's suggestion that Richard becomes an *alter Christus* in the context of the novel, p. 361.

[22] Cf. Frohock, p. 224; *Letters*, p. 181.

[23] Cf. Frohock, p. 225.

[24] Macdonald, p. 147.

[25] *A Death in the Family*, p. 290.

[26] Frohock, p. 227.

[27] Leslie Fiedler, "Encounter with Death," *New Republic*, CXXXVII (December 9, 1957), 26.

[28] Cf. Frohock, p. 228.

[29] Cf. Lewis, p. 51.

[30] *Let Us Now Praise Famous Men*, p. xv.

[31] Edward Ruhe, review of *A Death in the Family, Epoch*, VIII (Winter 1958), 249.

[32] Fiedler, p. 26.

[33] E. M. Forster, *Aspects of the Novel* (New York: Harcourt, Brace & World, Inc., Harvest Books, 1954), p. 6.

[34] Cf. the review by George P. Elliott, who confessed that he was not impressed because "some of my tears were jerked": "They're Dead But They Won't Lie Down," *Hudson Review*, XI (Spring 1958), 131–39; Elliott's remarks produced a defense of "sentimentality" from Gene Frumkin in "Editorial: A Sentimental Foray," *Coastlines*, no. 11 (Autumn 1958), 53–54.

[35] Ruhe, p. 249.

[36] Charles Feidelson, *Symbolism and American Literature*, p. 18.

[37] Cf. Hugh Kenner's remarks on Pound's *Cantos* as an open rather than closed field, in "Art in a Closed Field," *Virginia Quarterly Review*, XXXVIII (Autumn 1962), 609–13.

Chapter 6

[1] Macdonald, p. 152.

[2] *Ibid.*, p. 150.

[3] *Ibid.*, p. 154.

[4] *Ibid.*, p. 144.

[5] Frohock, p. 216.

[6] *Ibid.*, pp. 216–17.

[7] Robert Phelps, "James Agee," in *Letters,* p. 2.

[8] *Ibid.*, pp. 2–3.

[9] Alfred Kazin, "Good-by to James Agee," *Contemporaries* (Boston: Little, Brown and Company, 1962), pp. 185–86.

[10] John Updike, "No Use Talking," *New Republic,* CXLVII (August 13, 1962), 24.

[11] *Ibid.*

[12] Macdonald, p. 152.

[13] Walker Evans, "James Agee in 1936," *Let Us Now Praise Famous Men,* p. x.

[14] *Letters,* p. 72.

[15] Frohock, p. 216.

[16] *Let Us Now Praise Famous Men,* p. xvi.

[17] See Kenner's "Art in a Closed Field."

[18] F. W. Dupee, "The Prodigious James Agee," *New Leader,* XL (December 9, 1957), 21.

BIBLIOGRAPHY

I. PRIMARY SOURCES

A. Books by James Agee

Permit Me Voyage. New Haven: Yale University Press, 1934.

Let Us Now Praise Famous Men. Boston: Houghton Mifflin Co., 1941. Reprinted in 1960.

The Morning Watch. Boston: Houghton Mifflin Co., 1951.

A Death in the Family. New York: McDowell Obolensky, 1957.

Agee on Film: Reviews and Comments. New York: McDowell Obolensky, 1958.

Agee on Film, Vol. II: Five Film Scripts. New York: McDowell Obolensky, 1960.

The Letters of James Agee to Father Flye. New York: George Braziller, 1962.

B. Articles, poems, and short stories

"Boys Will Be Brutes," *Harvard Advocate*, CXVI (April 1930), 29–33.

"Good Friday," *Harvard Advocate*, CXVI (April 1930), 25.

"The Silver Sheet," *Harvard Advocate*, CXVI (April 1930), 42.

"Death in the Desert," *Harvard Advocate*, CXVII (October 1930), 16–24.

"Description of Elysium," *Harvard Advocate*, CXVII (March 1931), 18.

"You, Andrew Volstead," *Harvard Advocate*, CXVII (March 1931), 22–29.

"Resolution," *Harvard Advocate*, CXVII (May 1931), 77.

"Surburban Cawdor," *Harvard Advocate*, CXVII (May 1931), 86–88.

"They That Sow in Sorrow Shall Reap," *Harvard Advocate*, CXVII (May 1931), 9–23.

"The Truce," *Harvard Advocate*, CXVII (May 1931), 58–59.

"The Passionate Poet to His Love," in *The Harvard Advocate Anthology*, ed. Donald Hall. New York: Twayne Publishers, Inc., 1950. Dated February 1932.

"Sheep and Shuttleworths," *Fortune*, VII (January 1933), 43. Unsigned.

"A Poem of Poets," in *The Harvard Advocate Anthology*, pp. 229–230. Dated April 1933.

"The Poet's Valediction," in *The Harvard Advocate Anthology*. Dated April 1933.

"August in Saratoga," *Fortune*, VIII (August 1933), 63. Unsigned.

"The Project Is Important," *Fortune*, VIII (October 1931), 81. Unsigned.

"What D'You Mean, Modern?" *Fortune*, XII (November 1935), 97. Unsigned.

"The U.S. Commercial Orchid," *Fortune*, XII (December 1935), 108. Unsigned.

"Vertigral," *Saturday Review of Literature*, XIV (September 5, 1936), 9.

"Notes for a Moving Picture: The House," in *New Letters in America*, ed. Horace Gregory. New York: W. W. Norton & Company, 1937. 37–55.

"Lyrics," *Partisan Review*, IV (December 1937), 40–43.

"Rapid Transit," *Forum*, XCVI (February 1937), 115–16.

"Sun Our Father," *Forum*, XCVI (February 1937), 116.

"Six Days at Sea," *Fortune*, XVI (September 1937), 117. Unsigned.

"Summer Evening," *Harper's Monthly Magazine*, CLXXVI (January 1938), 205.

"Dixie Doodle," *Partisan Review*, IV (February 1938), 8.

"Song: I Had a Little Child," *Scholastic*, XXXIV (May 27, 1939), 27.

"Man's Fate—A Film Treatment of the Malraux Novel," *Films*, I (November 1939), 51–60.

"Europe: Autumn Story," *Time*, LXI (October 15, 1945), 24. Unsigned.

"Dedication Day," *Politics*, III (April 1946), 121–25. Reprinted in *New Directions*, vol. X, ed. James Laughlin. New Jersey: New Directions, 1948.

"Gandhi," *Politics*, V (Winter 1948), 4.

"Religion and the Intellectuals," *Partisan Review*, XVII (February 1950), 106–13.

"A Mother's Tale," *Harper's Bazaar*, LXXXVI (July (1952), 66–68; 102–107. Reprinted in *23 Modern Stories*, ed. Barbara Howes. New York: Vintage Books, 1963. 3–25

"Sunday: Outskirts of Knoxville, Tenn.," in Elizabeth Drew, *Poetry*. New York: Dell Publishing Co., Inc., 1959. 211–13.

II. SECONDARY SOURCES

Anon. "Agee on Agee," *Newsweek*, LX (July 23, 1962), 75.

—————. "In Love and Anger," *Time*, LXXVI (September 26, 1960), 112.

—————. "Rare Legacy of a Poet," *Life*, L (January 27, 1961), 96.

—————. Review of *Let Us Now Praise Famous Men*, *Newsweek*, LVI (September 5, 1960), 74.

—————. Review of *Agee on Film: Reviews and Comments*, *New Yorker*, XXXIV (December 13, 1958), 215.

—————. Review of *Let Us Now Praise Famous Men*, *Time*, XXXVIII (October 13, 1941), 104.

—————. "Unquiet One," *Time*, LXXX (August 3, 1962), 60.

Barker, George. "Three Tenant Families," *Nation*, CLIII (September 27, 1941), 282.

Benét, W. R. Review of *Permit Me Voyage*, *Saturday Review of Literature*, XI (November 24, 1934), 314.

Bingham, R. "Short of a Distant Goal," *Reporter*, XXVII (December 25, 1962), 54.

Bluestone, George. *Novels into Film*. Baltimore: The Johns Hopkins Press, 1957.

Bradbury, John. *Renaissance in the South*. Chapel Hill: University of North Carolina Press, 1963.

Breit, Harvey. Review of *Let Us Now Praise Famous Men*, *New Republic*, CV (September 15, 1941), 348–49.

Buber, Martin. *Eclipse of God*. New York: Harper & Brothers, 1957.

Chevalier, Haakon. "Translator's Introduction," in André

Malraux, *Man's Fate*. New York: Modern Library, 1936.

Cort, J. C. Review of *Let Us Now Praise Famous Men*, *Commonweal*, XXXIV (September 12, 1941), 499–500.

Crane, Stephen. *The Red Badge of Courage* and *Selected Prose and Poetry*, ed. William Gibson. New York: Holt, Rinehart and Winston, 1960.

Croce, Arlene. "Hollywood the Monolith," *Commonweal*, LXIX (January 23, 1959), 430–33.

Crowther, Bosley. Review of *Agee on Film: Reviews and Comments*, *American Scholar*, XXIX (Summer 1960), 436.

deFord, Miriam Allen. "Our Own American Inferno," *The Humanist*, XXI (January-February 1961), 55.

Dempsey, D. "Praise of Him Was Posthumous," *Saturday Review*, XLV (August 11, 1962), 24–25.

Drew, Elizabeth. *Poetry*. New York: Dell Publishing Co., Inc., 1959.

Dunlea, W. "Agee and the Writer's Vocation," *Commonweal*, LXXVI (September 7, 1962), 499–500.

Dupee, F. W. "The Prodigious James Agee," *New Leader*, XL (December 9, 1957), 20–21.

Elliott, George P. "They're Dead But They Won't Lie Down," *Hudson Review*, XI (Spring 1958), 131–39.

Empson, William. *Seven Types of Ambiguity*. New York: Meridian Books, 1958.

Etzkorn, L. R. Review of *Let Us Now Praise Famous Men*, *Library Journal*, LXVI (August 1941), 667.

Evans, Walker. "James Agee in 1936," *Atlantic*, CCVI (July 1960), 74–75. Included in the 1960 edition of *Let Us Now Praise Famous Men*.

Farber, Manny. "Star-Gazing for the Middlebrows," *New Leader*, XLI (December 8, 1958), 14–15.

————. "Underground Films," in *Film: An Anthology*,

ed. Donald Talbot. New York: Simon and Schuster, 1959.

Feidelson, Charles. *Symbolism and American Literature.* Chicago: University of Chicago Press, 1960.

Fiedler, Leslie. "Encounter with Death," *New Republic,* CXXXVII (December 9, 1957), 25–26.

Forster, E. M. *Aspects of the Novel.* New York: Harcourt Brace and World, Inc., Harvest Books, 1954.

Frohock, W. M. "James Agee—The Question of Wasted Talent," *The Novel of Violence in America.* Dallas: Southern Methodist University Press, 1957.

Frumkin, Gene. "Editorial: A Sentimental Foray," *Coastlines,* no. 11 (Autumn 1958), 53–54.

Goodman, Paul. Review of *Let Us Now Praise Famous Men, Partisan Review,* IX (January-February 1942), 86–87.

Griffith, Richard. Review of *Agee on Film: Reviews and Comments, New York Times Book Review* (November 16, 1958), p. 5.

Grossman, James. "Mr. Agee and the New Yorker," *Partisan Review,* XII (Winter 1945), 111–19.

Harker, Jonathan. Review of *Agee on Film: Reviews and Comments, Film Quarterly,* XII (Spring 1959), 58–61.

Hayes, R. "Rhetoric of Splendor," *Commonweal,* LXVIII (September 12, 1958), 591–92.

Hicks, Granville. "Suffering Face of the Rural South," *Saturday Review,* XLIII (September 10, 1960), 19–20.

Holland, Norman. "Agee on Film: Reviewer Re-Viewed," *Hudson Review,* XII (Spring 1959), 148–51.

Huston, John. "Introduction," *Agee on Film, Vol. II: Five Film Scripts.* New York: McDowell Obolensky, 1960.

Kauffmann, Stanley. "Life in Reviews," *New Republic,* CXXXIX (December 1, 1958), 18–19.

Kazin, Alfred. *Contemporaries.* Boston: Little, Brown and Co., 1962.

—————. *On Native Grounds.* New York: Reynal and Hitchcock, 1942.

Kenner, Hugh. "Art in a Closed Field," *Virginia Quarterly Review,* XXXVIII (Autumn 1962), 585–613.

Kirstein, Lincoln. "First Poems," *New Republic,* LXXXII (February 27, 1935), 80–81.

Knight, Arthur. Review of *Agee on Film: Reviews and Comments, Saturday Review,* XLI (December 20, 1958), 9.

Larsen, E. "Let Us Not Now Praise Ourselves," *Carleton Miscellany,* II (Winter 1961), 86–96.

Lechlitner, Ruth. "Alabama Tenant Families," *New York Herald Tribune Book Review,* (August 24, 1941), p. 10.

Lewis, R. W. S. *The American Adam.* Chicago: University of Chicago Press, 1959.

Lewis, Wyndham. *The Letters of Wyndham Lewis,* ed. W. K. Rose. London: Methuen & Co., Ltd., 1963.

Macdonald, Dwight. *Against the American Grain.* New York: Random House, 1962.

Malraux, André. *Man's Fate.* New York: Modern Library, 1936.

Mann, Charles W., Jr. Review of *Agee on Film: Reviews and Comments, Library Journal,* LXXXIII (December 15, 1958), 3509.

McCord, David. Review of *Permit Me Voyage, Yale Review,* n.s. XXIV (Winter 1935), 394.

Miller, James E., Jr. *A Critical Guide to Leaves of Grass.* Chicago: University of Chicago Press, 1957.

—————, Karl Shapiro and Bernice Slote. *Start With the Sun.* Lincoln: University of Nebraska Press, 1960.

Nichols, Dudley. *Twenty Best Film Plays,* ed. with John Gassner. New York: Crown, 1943.

Oulahan, Richard. "A Cult Grew Around a Many-Sided Writer," *Life*, LV (November 1, 1963), 69–72.

P., C. G. Review of *Permit Me Voyage*, *New York Times Book Review* (December 30, 1934), p. 10.

Panofsky, Erwin. "Style and Medium in the Moving Pictures," in *Films An Anthology*, ed. Donald Talbot. New York: Simon and Schuster, 1959.

Phelps, Robert. "James Agee," in *The Letters of James Agee to Father Flye*. New York: George Braziller, 1962.

Phillipson, J. S. "Character, Theme, and Symbol in *The Morning Watch*," *Western Humanities Review*, XV (Autumn 1961), 359–67.

Robertson, Priscilla. "Agee's Special View," *Progressive*, XXV (January 1961), 44–45.

Rodman, Seldon (ed.), *One Hundred Modern Poems*, New York: New American Library, 1949.

Rodman, Seldon. Review of *Let Us Now Praise Famous Men*, *Saturday Review of Literature*, XXIV (August 23, 1941), 6.

Rosenberg, Harold. "Insurrections," *New Yorker*, XL (March 14, 1964), 169–88.

————. "The New as Value," *New Yorker*, XXXIX (September 7, 1963), 136–46.

————. *The Tradition of the New*. New York: Grove Press, 1961.

Ruhe, Edward. Review of *A Death in the Family*, *Epoch*, VIII (Winter 1958), 247–51.

Sarris, Andrew. "The American Cinema," *Film Culture*, no. 28 (Spring 1963), 1–68.

————. "The Auteur Theory," *Film Quarterly*, XVI (Summer 1963), 26–33.

Sayers, Dorothy. *The Mind of the Maker*. New York: Living Age Books, 1959.

Schorer, Mark. "Technique as Discovery," in *Forms of*

Modern Fiction, ed. William Van O'Connor. Minneapolis: University of Minnesota Press, 1948.

Scott, Winfield T. Review of *Agee on Film: Reviews and Comments*, *New York Herald Tribune Book Review*, (February 15, 1959), p. 12.

——————. Review of *Let Us Now Praise Famous Men*, *New York Herald Tribune Book Review* (October 9, 1960), p. 6.

Thornton, Richard (ed.), *Recognition of Robert Frost*, New York: Henry Holt and Company, 1932.

Updike, John. "No Use Talking," *New Republic*, CXLVII (August 13, 1962), 23–24.

Wald, Jerry. "Screen Adaptation," *Films in Review*, V (February 1954), 62–67.

Walton, E. L. Review of *Permit Me Voyage*, *New York Herald Tribune Book Review* (December 9, 1934), p. 19.

Weales, G. "The Critic in Love," *Reporter*, XIX (December 25, 1958), 38–39.

Wensberg, Erik. "Celebration, Adoration and Wonder," *Nation*, CLXXII (November 26, 1960), 417–18.

Whitman, Walt. *An American Primer*, ed. Horace Traubel. Boston: Small, Maynard, 1904.

——————. *The Complete Writings of Walt Whitman*, ed. Richard M. Bucke et al. New York: G. P. Putnam's Sons, 1902.

——————. *Leaves of Grass*, ed. Emory Holloway, Inclusive Edition. Garden City, N. Y.: Doubleday, 1925.

Wimsatt, W. K., Jr. *The Verbal Icon*. New York: The Noonday Press, 1960.

Winters, Yvor. *In Defense of Reason*. New York: The Swallow Press and W. Morrow & Co., 1947.

Young, Vernon. "Film Chronicle," *Hudson Review*, XIV (Summer 1961), 270–73.